THE
—BLACKWELL—
GUIDE TO
WALL STREET

THE —BLACKWELL— GUIDE TO WALL STREET

Bluford H. Putnam and Sandra C. Zimmer

Basil Blackwell

First published 1987

Basil Blackwell Ltd
108 Cowley Road, Oxford OX4 1JF, UK

Basil Blackwell Inc.
432 Park Avenue South, Suite 1503,
New York, NY 10016, USA

British Library Cataloguing in Publication Data

Putnam, Bluford H.
The Blackwell guide to Wall Street
1. Finance
I. Title II. Zimmer, Sandra C.
332   HG173
ISBN 0–631–14183–9

Library of Congress Cataloging in Publication Data

Putnam, Bluford H.
The Blackwell guide to Wall Street.

Includes index.
1. Securities—United States. 2. Investments—
United States. I. Zimmer, Sandra C. II. Title.
HG4910.P87 1987   332.63'2   87–10299
ISBN 0–631–14183–9

Typeset in 10 on 12pt Garamond
by Opus, Oxford
Printed in Great Britain by TJ Press Ltd, Padstow

This volume is dedicated to our parents:
Dorothy Page and B. Hugh Putnam, and Ann Lee
and Merle V. Zimmer.

Contents

Preface

Some observers of Wall Street see tall buildings, large brokerage houses, big banks, the American and New York Stock Exchanges, or regulatory authorities such as the Securities and Exchange Commission. From this perspective come books about the institutions of Wall Street.

To us, however, Wall Street is not buildings and institutions. Rather, it is the center of an exciting marketplace – a marketplace of ideas. The degree of innovation, in terms of new products and improved concepts, is at a fever-pitch level. Times were not always like this on Wall Street. Revolutions in technology, market deregulation, and increasingly volatile economic events have forced changes in traditional business practices.

Ideas are now at a premium. And this Guide to Wall Street is a tour through some of the more important concepts that one needs to understand in order to grasp how risk is priced and returns are earned in today's financial markets. No investor and no corporation is exempt from the profound forces of change that are sweeping world financial markets, and we hope this volume contributes to the understanding of this evolving world.

Bluford H. Putnam
Sandra C. Zimmer

Acknowledgements

The authors would like to thank several individuals and institutions for their contributions to this effort.

While this book is not intended for an audience of academic scholars, the material presented here is derived from a large body of accepted thought on how markets work. Many well-known scholars have contributed to this body of knowledge and they are not explicitly recognized. This does not diminish our debt to them, and we want to acknowledge our thanks to academia.

More specifically, we are grateful to Joel Stern and the corporate finance advisory and management services firm of which he is the president, Stern Stewart & Company. Joel has provided intellectual guidance, which surfaces throughout the book. Also, we want to thank Stern Stewart & Company for permission to reprint material prepared initially for publication of the firm.

Individually, our thanks especially go to Donald Chew, David Glassman, Mark Gressle, Louis Hall, John Paulus, Eric Seff, Clifford Smith, Alden Toevs, Sykes Wilford, and J. Richard Zecher for their ideas on various topics which found their way into this book.

In addition, we appreciate the assistance of Meryl Lantner and Stephanie Otten in preparing this volume.

Disclaimer

Introduction:
Revolution on Wall Street

Over the past two decades, Wall Street has been swept by forces that have had a dramatic impact on global financial markets. As a result of these changes, it has become more competitive, more efficient, and more innovative.

Evidence of the profound nature of these changes can be seen in every aspect of Wall Street. Competitive markets have forced weaker firms to the side and have encouraged the stronger firms to consolidate their positions. For example, more than 30 firms went into the making of Shearson Lehman/American Express. The consolidated firms included some impressive names – Shearson Hayden Stone, Hornblower and Weeks, Kuhn Loeb, and Lehman Brothers, among others.

Other firms have grown from the inside. Take the case of Morgan Stanley and Company. This firm was formed from the J. P. Morgan banking empire after the enactment of the Glass–Steagall Act in the United States in the 1930s which prevented commercial banks from underwriting stock and bond issues for corporate clients. After over 30 years of highly profitable and distinguished business, the firm was still a tightly held partnership in 1969 with no more than 300 employees and less than $10 million in capital. By 1986, however, Morgan Stanley and Company had grown to over 4000 employees in offices around the world, could boast of over $1 billion in capital and had offered a portion of its shares to the public.

Another example can be found in the form of discount brokers, which were not even allowed before stock market commissions were deregulated in the early 1970s. Now they execute between 15 and 20 percent of the public's stock transactions, charging significantly lower commissions than regular brokers.

Meanwhile, individual investors have diminished in importance as institutional money managers, such as pension funds, have grown. These fund managers are also proving to be very active traders. Estimates have been made that more than 60 percent of the shares in professionally managed portfolios are turned over each year. The professionals also trade in size. Trades of more than 10,000 shares, known as block trades, accounted for less than 20 percent of market activity in 1975, but in 1985 block trading accounted for half of the market's volume.

Documenting these changes is easy. The signs are everywhere, and Wall Street has clearly undergone a major revolution. Understanding the cause of this revolution, however, requires a close examination of a number of key forces. These winds of change, which have been dominated by three major forces, are what this book is all about.

Institutionalization, Information, and Risk

The first major cause for change has been the institutionalization of the market as pension funds, trust funds, insurance companies, and other large institutions have come to displace the individual investor as the driving force in our stock, bond, and money markets. This development has been associated with substantial improvements in the pension plans offered to most workers. As these plans accumulated large sums of money in the 1960s and 1970s, they became the key players on Wall Street.

A second major impetus for change has come about by way of significantly reduced information costs. The ability of the financial system to gather information about the economy, corporations, and government policies has been greatly enhanced by the technological revolution. The introduction and rapid assimilation of personal computers, innovations in word processing, and breakthroughs in telephone and video communications have all meant that the institutions involved in trading securities now have very cheap access to information that 10, 20, and 30 years ago was very costly to obtain. Widespread availability of inexpensive and extremely timely information has improved the market's ability to price risk efficiently and quickly.

This enhanced ability to price risks has been of critical importance given the third major change that has swept Wall Street. This change has to do with a shift in both the type and the severity of risks facing the market. In particular, the last two decades have seen a major increase in the risks faced by financial market participants.

This increase in risk has been associated with five factors: (1) the rampant rise in inflation during the 1970s and a resulting inflation risk, (2) the floating of exchange rates in the early 1970s and subsequent foreign exchange risk facing global investors, (3) substantial changes in the prices of commodities relative to the prices of other goods and services, with the most visible of these being the oil price shocks of 1974 and 1979 and their reversal in the 1980s, (4) the higher probability of bankruptcy in various parts of the global economy, which has increased the risk of credit disruption and forced the world's banking and financial systems to deal with a much greater probability of bankruptcy than ever before; and, finally, (5) important changes in tax laws. The probability of rapid changes in the future has forced markets to deal with a high degree of uncertainty as to what the rules of the game will be over the next several years. Rapidly changing tax laws were not a feature of the 1950s and 1960s. Not knowing what the rules will be has made playing the game much, much harder and riskier.

The Wall Street Response

As a consequence of the institutionalization of the market, declines in the cost of processing information, and changes in the risks faced by the market, there have been profound changes in how Wall Street operates. The most basic change has been in the way risks are shifted from one party to another.

Because of the large increases and changes in risk, individuals and corporations have often found themselves bearing certain risks for which they were unsuited. In turn, they have sought ways to shift undesirable risks to other parties who are more willing to accept or manage these risks. The method utilized by Wall Street to accomplish this shift is known as 'securitization' (noun, changed to a verb, and used as a gerund). Through this process, a commercial bank can take particular loans which it considers to be riskier than when originally booked, package them into a security, and trade them to another bank, a pension fund, or some other set of investors. The price at which this transaction takes place will clearly reflect the higher risks associated with the 1970s and 1980s. Commercial banks do not avoid the loss of having made the original mistake in accessing risk, but they are better able to construct and adjust their portfolio, such that in the future the institution takes on only the risk it desires.

Innovation

The securitization of the market has spawned a major push toward innovation as substantial rewards have been made available to those who could invent new tools – new securities that package risks in a manner more suitable to the types of risks faced by the market in this changing environment. A prime example of innovation can be seen in the futures markets. Financial futures have gone from virtually ground zero with the first offering of contracts in mortgage-backed securities (in the early 1970s) to contracts which include foreign exchange, bonds, Treasury bills, and Eurodollars. More recently, we have seen permutations of these instruments, such as options on futures as well as bond issues with warrants attached which give the investor an option to buy future bonds at specified prices.

All of these innovations accomplish the same thing. They repackage risk. By segregating various risks into different packages, they can not only be priced more accurately, but can also allow investors to pick and choose the types of risks they want to accept. In addition, investors can more accurately calculate the return they must get for accepting these types of risks.

Globalization

These trends have not been limited to Wall Street. They are happening on a global basis. Another consequence of declining information costs, rising institutionalization, and worldwide changes in risks is that markets around the world are more closely linked than ever before. The innovations that have occurred in the United States have been followed in the City of London and in the financial districts of the Far East – Singapore, Tokyo, and Hong Kong. Sometimes innovations have started in European or Asian markets and made their way to the United States, and other times the United States has been the innovator. But whatever the direction of change, all markets around the globe adjust very quickly. In this closely linked world, there are few time lags in the securities markets.

Deregulation

The trends of globalization and securitization have also been associated with the deregulation of financial markets. This deregulation has occurred primarily because the costs of working in a rigid framework in the face of new and rising risks were too great. The incentive to develop tools to circumvent old rigidities was extremely high. Thus, the market's reaction to increased risks started the deregulation process rolling. Furthermore, globalization has served to increase the deregulation tempo because investors, corporations, and other entities operating in a highly regulated market have found it relatively easy to set up another market outside the bounds of that country. A classic example of this is the development of the Euromarket, largely outside of the regulation of US authorities such as the Federal Reserve or US Treasury.

The growth of these less regulated markets has forced governments to reconsider both their regulations and the manner in which institutions are monitored. In short, governments have not been on the leading edge of deregulation. They have merely been reacting to global forces – and the market's response to these forces. What governments have found is that the only way a country can compete successfully in this new age is to allow its financial markets as much flexibility as possible.

As a consequence, the deregulation move around the world has been impressive. Foreign banks are now allowed to compete with domestic banks in Australia. The Stock Exchange in London is de-fixing commissions. The Ministry of Finance and the Bank of Japan are changing Japanese securities markets, liberalizing them to allow more foreign participation; and authorities in Germany have opened their bond markets to allow for floating-rate notes and zero-coupon bonds denominated in German marks.

These are just a few examples of how countries are being forced to respond to innovations in the markets. The net result has been a sharp increase in the growth of securities markets around the world.

Implications

There are a number of important implications resulting from these changes. First, there is better risk management. The new tools available for managing risks – futures, options, warrants – all allow the corporation or the investor to pick and choose risks more carefully. Needless to say, improved risk management is not free. The premium, for instance, of capping the interest rate on a loan so that it will not rise above a certain level if market interest rates rise is not cheap. This is one of the costs associated with a risky world. Of course, the economy as a whole is much better off by paying these costs. The economy would have to pay an even higher price without this improved risk management, which allows institutions and individuals to cope with their increasingly risky world.

The second consequence is that corporate management has come under increasing pressure to perform. As risk management techniques have improved the market pricing of risks, stock and bond prices have become better gauges for management performance. As a result, management is being held to higher standards.

One aspect of this has been the trend toward large corporate restructurings. These restructurings have been accomplished largely through either mergers or internal restructuring of a corporation's capital base, whereby more debt has been issued and in some cases equity has been repurchased by the corporation. The net result has been corporations with higher debt/equity ratios. This has occurred in the United States because it has been shown that greater use of debt (because the interest is tax-deductible) can raise stock prices.

In the energy sector, there has been tremendous activity in terms of acquisitions – many of them hostile in nature. Corporate raiders have perceived that the managements of certain energy companies were not taking full advantage of their resources or of the tax laws, and, in short, were not maximizing value for their shareholders. Through means which are often subject to bitter debate and legal challenges, corporate raiders have forced managements to recognize their shortcomings and to manage their businesses with the maximization of shareholder wealth as a more direct objective.

Not only has corporate management come under increasing pressure, but governments are being disciplined as well. Changes in government policy can have profound effects on interest rates, exchange rates, and stock prices. The intensity with which corporations and investors scrutinize government policies and then act on them by buying or selling securities has been rising. And as a result, the market evaluates government policies quickly and efficiently. Governments that take widely divergent paths can see exchange rates respond immediately. These responses signal the consequences of governmental actions much more quickly than in the 1950s and 1960s.

For instance, when the socialists took control of the government in France in 1981, and President Mitterand initiated a number of socialist policies which were clearly designed to expand the economy at a rapid rate, the market judged that this expansion was too fast and that the new structures were too rigid and would not work. As as result, the French franc sank dramatically on the foreign exchange markets and inflation in France began to rise. A similar reaction was seen in the United States in 1979, when the Federal Reserve System adopted a tight monetary policy and became convinced that following monetary targets was essential to controlling inflation. The world was thrown into a deep, two-year recession, and the subsequent effect on world inflation is still being felt.

In short, markets and governments interact much more quickly today than they ever have. When governments change their policies, therefore, they must not only look to the effect on voters, but must also analyze the likely effect in the financial markets and how this market effect may change the way the policy will actually work.

A fourth implication has been that investors are finding it harder and harder to find underpriced securities. Because the markets process information so quickly and can price risks efficiently, it is difficult to find investments that would yield unusually large returns at low risk. Certainly it has always been true there has been no free lunch on Wall Street and no easy money made, but changes in the last two decades have made it even more difficult for professional investors to outperform market standards. That is to say, highly paid professional money managers who run large pension funds are finding it increasingly difficult to outperform stock indexes such as the S&P 500. As this has occurred, many pension and other institutional funds are indexing their portfolios to guarantee that they will do as well as a given market standard like the S&P 500. Of course, if the S&P 500 is down 10 percent, they will be down 10 percent too. If it is up 15 percent they will be up 15 percent. They will do literally the same as the market. The inability to outperform the market and the ability to set up portfolios that index the market is one of the major effects of the changes that have been sweeping across Wall Street.

The final implication of all these changes is perhaps the most important. It has to do with the fact that corporate managers, individual investors, and portfolio managers must now think on a global basis. When Japan raised its interest rates dramatically in October 1985, the bond market in New York fell sharply the same day. When the United States changed monetary policy in 1979 and held to that policy in 1980, 1981, and 1982, it changed the course of the dollar for five years and sent the world into a disinflation path that affected the ability of Latin American governments to pay their debts. It also dramatically reduced the wealth of OPEC as downward pressure was brought to bear on oil prices for the first time since the OPEC crisis of 1974 and 1979. These are global factors, and they sweep back and forth across the world.

A person investing only in US bonds must now realize that the return he is going to get may be affected by events in Bonn, London, or Tokyo. Events in these financial centers can affect how the Federal Reserve managers monitor monetary policy, which in turn can affect the path of interest rates in the United States. In short, there is no such thing as a purely domestic investor or corporation any more. Every investor and every corporation faces global risk and must analyze problems on a global basis.

The winds of change that we have discussed – the institutionalization of the market, the decline of information costs, and the change and increase in risks facing businesses and investors – require us to look very closely at two related topics. The first is the relationship between risk and return. It is axiomatic that higher risks require higher return. Since Wall Street is in the business of pricing risks and trading risks from one investor to another, the first step in understanding Wall Street and the revolution going on there is to develop an understanding of the relationship between risk and return. This is the topic of chapter 1.

The second critical issue is market efficiency – how markets incorporate expectations of future events and how this affects the paths of stock prices, interest rates, foreign exchange, and commodities. Chapter 2 therefore focuses on market efficiency and the dynamics of prices. It is important to understand how the market incorporates projections of future events and determines the probabilities that an event will occur. How risks are priced affects the price of shares, bonds, and all other securities.

The first two chapters set the framework for understanding the markets of Wall Street – how Wall Street assesses risk and return, how expectations of the future are incorporated into the returns that investors are offered.

With this background, the rest of the book is divided into three major parts: the stock market, the fixed-income or bond markets, and foreign exchange markets.

In part II a number of corporate finance topics will be covered. Once one understands how the market assesses value and prices risk, one can then ask the question in a different form. In short, what is a corporation worth and how is it valued? From this question, and the answer to it, other issues in corporate financial management can be raised and discussed. For example, what is the appropriate debt/equity ratio for a corporation? How does one assess mergers and acquisitions? What is an appropriate dividend policy for a corporation? The answers to these questions are plugged back into the process of valuing a corporation, which is what Wall Street does every day and every minute in the stock market. And, since much of a stock's value depends on future projections of how much money a corporation can make and how risky that projection is, we are going to come back to the themes of risk, return, efficiency, and dynamics.

Part III opens with a chapter describing the critical links between bonds and stocks. In many ways, developments in interest rates drive the stock market up and down, and this relationship is given special attention. Other topics in this part include yield curves, duration analysis, and real interest rates. In every case, though, the key concepts revolve around the proper pricing of risks.

The key that links the stock and bond markets of separate countries into highly integrated, global markets is a huge market in its own right – foreign exchange. Over $300 billion worth of currency transactions occur daily, from Tokyo to London to New York, in this 24-hour global market. Part IV investigates this market and provides a conceptual basis for understanding how foreign exchange markets tie the world together and what makes them tick.

In the final analysis, all of us, individuals and corporations, are in the business of allocating capital. When we borrow money or when we invest we are assessing risks and expected returns. Wall Street is in the business of allocating capital. And, as we have seen, the business of allocating capital is more complicated and more challenging than it has ever been.

The focus of this book is to provide a framework for analyzing how Wall Street allocates capital. The last two decades have seen powerful winds force revolutionary changes on Wall Street and financial markets around the world. The concepts investigated in the book are important building blocks for understanding why the changes have taken place and how these efficient, global markets operate. They also provide insights into where financial markets are headed, and thoughts on this subject are contained in the book's concluding chapter.

Part I
Basic Concepts

1

No Guts, No Glory:
The Economics of Risk and Return

The relationship between risk and return is probably the most important concept underlying financial markets. In essence, Wall Street is in the business of allocating capital based on risk and return criteria. The basic premise is that a rational investor expects to be compensated with higher returns when accepting riskier investments. For our purposes, *risk** is defined as the possibility that our expectations will not be realized.

In this chapter we are going to look at the question of risk and return in three different ways. Initially, the basic principles of risk and return analysis will be discussed. The tradeoff between risk and return is actually a very simple concept, but since it will be applied continually throughout this book it must be understood thoroughly. Next, we will take a look at the pricing of avoidable risks. Certain investment opportunities contain risks that may be offset by the risks associated with other investment opportunities. By buying both investments, the risk structure of the combined investment portfolio will be quite different from a portfolio involving only one of the investments. The concept of avoidable risks is essentially the concept of portfolio diversification. Finally, we will look at risk and risk preferences that are not symmetrical. A particular investor may prefer to limit down-side risk and still maintain the opportunity for substantial gain. Certain types of securities possess this type of asymmetry. Thus, asymmetrical risk can be achieved – at a price. The point here is that in analyzing an investment one has to look not only at its return and risk, but also at the distribution of the risk.

*Terms appearing in the Glossary (see p.195) are italicized in the text when first used.

Risk and Return

One of the principle lessons of economics is that virtually
everything one decides to do in life involves a tradeoff. The decision
to take a vacation at the beach is made by weighing all the other
possibilities, such as a vacation in the mountains or a trip to Europe.
When one decides between various alternatives, one assesses both
the characteristics and the price of each possibility. Investors on
Wall Street focus on two key characteristics. The first is the
expected return of an investment – how much money will I make?
The second is how risky the investment is – what are the chances
that I will lose money or that I will make a greater return than
expected?

The basic principle behind the risk – return tradeoff is illustated
in figure 1.1. Here the vertical axis measures expected return and the
horizontal axis, risk. The upward-sloping line describes the
risk–return tradeoff. Moving to the right from point *A* to point *B*
involves an increase in both return and risk. The return from an
investment at point *B* is substantially higher than the return on
investment *A*; the associated risk is also higher.

Notice that point *C* represents an investment which has a return
substantially above the standard risk–return tradeoff. *C* thus
represents an extremely attractive investment because it is earning
returns well in excess of other investments with similar risk. As

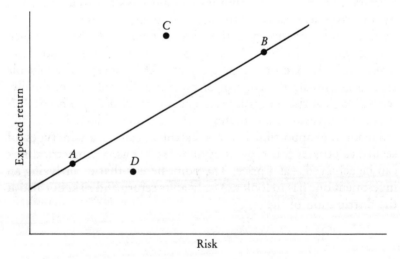

Figure 1.1   Risk vs. return tradeoff

investors discover this investment, they will buy it, bidding up its price and thereby lowering its expected return. New investors will find that point C is moving rapidly down toward the line, because as the price of investment C rises they will not have the same opportunity to earn excessive returns.

Point D, on the other hand, represents an asset with returns that cannot be justified by the risk involved. As investors who hold asset D realize this, some of them will sell the asset and its price will fall. As the price of investment D falls, a point will be reached where there is enough potential price appreciation and expected return to justify the risks being taken. That is, point D will move upwards toward the line. If you happen to own investment D while this adjustment process is going on you will lose money, because you will have invested in an asset which did not earn sufficient returns to compensate you for the risk involved.

Not surprisingly, the basic goal of a securities professional is to discover over- and undervalued securities, finding investment opportunities like point C while avoiding investment opportunities like point D. Along a similar vein, the goal of a portfolio manager is to put together a set of investments which, taken together, will produce a targeted risk–return tradeoff. Of course, the goals of portfolio managers may differ. Portfolio managers investing funds for a pension plan may have relatively low-risk portfolio criteria as specified by the owners of the pension plan. In this case, the goal would be to put together an investment portfolio that is closer to point A. Other investors may seek to take more risks and earn the higher returns associated with it.

Corporations, too, have to live by the risk and return tradeoffs that we have described here. Imagine a corporation that has four different lines of business: divisions A, B, C, and D, corresponding to the points on our risk–return graph. Division A could be considered a business that generates a steady flow of profits year-in and year-out, but whose profits are relatively low. Division B does not exhibit a steady flow of profits; there are some good years and some bad years. However, the good years have very high profits, and, over a reasonable period of time, division B has proven to be very profitable, even with the higher risks inherent in this particular line of business. Division C is the star. It consistently earns very high profits without much variability in earnings from year to year. Division D is the poor performer. Profitability is both low and variable, implying that the risks are very high.

A corporation looking at these four divisions would probably want to consider either restructuring division D, or changing its management – or perhaps selling the whole division, because it is not earning its way, given the risks. By the same token, division C is a candidate for expansion. It is earning excess returns relative to the risks being taken. Perhaps there are ways that this division can be expanded without lowering returns. Later in the book we will discuss a series of corporate finance issues, but as the preceding example suggests, these discussions will start with a basic understanding of the tradeoff between risk and return.

In summary, one of the key principles of risk versus return is that higher returns are generally associated with higher risks. However, a key factor on Wall Street is whether or not the risk involved can be avoided.

Avoidable Risks

When an investor buys shares in a corporation he does not buy them in isolation. He adds them to the portfolio he already owns. Investors, therefore, should not just be assessing the risk of any one share; they must look at the risk of their entire portfolio. Thus, when a new company's shares are added to the portfolio or old ones are removed, it is extremely important to assess how these decisions change the risk and return characteristics of the portfolio as a whole.

This assessment is important because a number of risks are diversifiable. That is, portfolios can be constructed where the risk of one investment offsets the risk of another. If an event occurs, the price of one share may go up while the price of the other may fall. Such a portfolio is hedged or protected

Understanding the principles of offsetting risks and diversifying a portfolio adds a new dimension to understanding how Wall Street prices risk. Wall Street will not pay for a risk that can be avoided. Similarly, it will always extract a premium for unavoidable risk.

One can think of different kinds of risk. First, there is the risk that the economy will go into recession or have a boom year. This might be referred to as the risk of the market or the whole economy. Then there is industry risk. The oil industry did exceedingly well in the 1970s, but with energy prices falling it is not doing very well in the 1980s. The technology industries have performed quite differently from the energy industry, and the housing industry has behaved differently still. Thus, industry risk is a separate category. Finally, one must consider company risk. There may be 15 companies in a given industry. Depending on the quality of management in each company, one company may outperform another even if the industry as a whole does well or poorly. Company-specific risk can also involve such things as a warehouse fire, embezzlement, or expropriated assets – disasters that are unpredictable, one-time events in a company's history.

The risk of the entire economy having a good year or bad year is not a diversifiable risk. One is stuck with how the economy performs. However, the risks of different industries can be diversified. One does not need to hold a portfolio just of oil shares: one can buy ten oil companies for a portfolio and also ten computer firms, five food retailers, and maybe some paper industry companies. In other words, the portfolio can be diversified across companies and industries, limiting the ups and downs of the whole portfolio by owning more than one type of industry. So, to a certain extent, industry risk can be diversified.

Company-specific risk is the type of risk that is most easily avoided through diversification. By buying a number of companies within an industry, one's portfolio will likely move up or down as the industry does well or poorly. By buying ten or more companies within an industry, one will pick a few star performers and a few poor or disaster-struck performers, ending up with the average performance of the industry. In this way, the risk that one company will outperform or underperform the average of its industry is avoided.

This has certain implications for how Wall Street prices shares for different companies. Suppose, for instance, that a very large company decides to expand into a totally new business. In effect, the company is diversifying across industries. For example, a company in the steel industry may decide to purchase a company in the oil industry. The question that Wall Street asks is, What does this do for me? I already own a portfolio of oil stocks and steel stocks. I can do that diversification myself. So diversification across industries is not likely to help the stock price of the company, even though it may have the effect of stabilizing the earnings of the combined enterprise. What Wall Street *will* pay for, however, are improvements that give the firm an ability to outperform other companies within its industry.

There is obviously more to examples such as these, and we will continue this discussion in a later chapter which focuses on mergers and acquisitions. The point is that understanding the risks that Wall Street can diversify on its own is key to understanding what will happen to a share price when a company chooses to do some of this diversification itself. If Wall Street has already been able to avoid a certain risk, it is not likely to pay for someone else to avoid that risk.

The measurement of risk, in the sense of market or systematic risk that cannot be diversified and company-specific or unsystematic risks that are diversifiable, is a key concept. The measurement that Wall Street uses is referred to as *beta*. Beta measures how a company or an industry performs relative to the market as a whole. The market in this sense represents the entire stock market and has, by definition, a beta equal to one. A beta exceeding 1 – 1.5 for example – indicates that the industry or the company is one and a half times more volatile that the market as a whole; that is, if the market is up 10 percent in a year, a stock with a beta of 1.5 would be expected to have increased 15 percent in price. By the same token, if the market were down 10 percent, one would expect the stock with a beta of 1.5 to be down 15 percent. A beta of less than 1 suggests an industry or a company that produces returns that are more stable than the market as a whole. If the market were up 10 percent, the company with a beta of 0.8 would be up only 8 percent; if the market were down 10 percent, the company would be down only 8 percent. A low beta, or a beta of less than one, indicates a very stable flow of earnings year-in, year-out.

Some examples of this concept may be useful. For instance, the food industries are considered low-beta industries. People always eat – in a recession they eat, in a boom they eat. Companies like General Foods or Coca Cola generally have a beta of less than one. A high-beta company or industry might be the airline industry. When the economy is doing well people take more vacations – they travel more, and the industry booms. When the economy does poorly, businesses cut back on discretionary travel, consumers do not take as many vacations, and airlines do even more poorly than the economy as a whole. Thus, airlines are considered a high-beta industry.

Furthermore, not all companies in the same industry may have the same beta. A classic example of this is the computer industry. This industry is dominated by one company, known as 'Big Blue' or IBM. IBM has a different beta from other companies in the industry because it sets industry standards in many product lines. Thus, it is a lower-risk company and has a lower beta. Other companies have all the risks that IBM has plus one more: they have IBM risk. If IBM chooses to introduce a new product line, all the other companies in the industry are faced with having to respond. This makes for a risky business. So, even within an industry, the beta of different companies can vary.

Now how does one use beta? Figure 1.2 looks very much like the risk–return graph in the preceding section. Interspersed on the figure are the estimated betas, as a measure of risk, for certain industries. The food industry is on the low-risk side; the airlines up there are the high-risk industry. And as you can see, the returns that one would expect from owning airline stocks versus food stocks are quite different. Airline stocks are expected to provide larger total returns – dividends and capital gains – than food stocks.

Thus we see how beta provides a measure of risk for companies and industries. Furthermore, by analyzing the betas of stocks in a portfolio, it is possible to derive a beta for the portfolio as a whole. Depending on one's risk preferences, low- or high-beta portfolios may be desired. The key issue is that offsetting risks within the portfolio need to be examined; therefore, individual stock choices should not be viewed in isolation.

Another way to look at offsetting risks and portfolio diversification is to take the example of gold. Gold is an investment that dances to a different drummer. Because of this, a small piece of gold

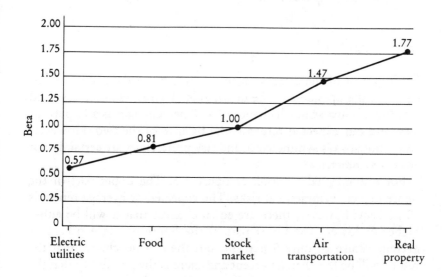

Figure 1.2 Industry riskiness

(*Source:* Barr Rosenberg and Andrew Rudd, 'The Corporate Uses of Beta,' *Issues in Corporate Finance*, Stern Stewart & Co., New York, 1983.)

added to a large portfolio has a tendency to stabilize the return expected from the overall portfolio. Most other investments respond in the same direction as the market but by different magnitudes. Gold sometimes goes the other way. As a result, many global investors hold 5 percent or some small proportion of their total portfolio in gold as a hedge. On the other hand, if one held a portfolio of 100 percent gold, it would be one of the most risky investments around. The idea that gold can be both a risky investment and a hedge may not be intuitive, but it should be clear that there is a world of difference between keeping 5 percent of one's wealth in gold and 100 percent of one's wealth in gold. Because it often moves in the opposite direction, holding 5 percent of a portfolio in gold can actually help to stabilize the other 95 percent of a diversified portfolio in terms of total return.

Understanding these differences is what modern portfolio theory is about and is a key aspect of how Wall Street prices both risks and securities. The question is not just how risky the investment is, but also how that risk fits in with the other risks in a portfolio. That is, what risks are avoidable or can be neutralized by offsetting risks in a portfolio? This is the issue of portfolio *diversification*, which we will be coming back to time and again to show how it affects the way Wall Street prices risk.

Asymmetry of Risk

During most of the discussion so far, risk has been assumed to be equal on the up-side and the down-side. That is, we have assumed that there is just as much chance of a 10 percent gain as a 10 percent loss, and our expected return is the balance of the two. However, risk is not always symmetrical, and risk preferences are certainly not always symmetrical.

For example, take a look at figure 1.3. The upper part of the figure depicts symmetrical risks. The expected or average return is 10 percent; however, there are equal chances that it will be either higher or lower. The lower part of the figure has an expected or average return of only 9 percent, but there is no chance that the return will be less than 6 percent and there is the possibility that the return will exceed 12 percent. If you had a choice between either of these investment portfolios, which one would you take? The answer is not obvious. It depends on your risk preferences. If having to bear the full brunt of the down-side risk has a very high cost to you,

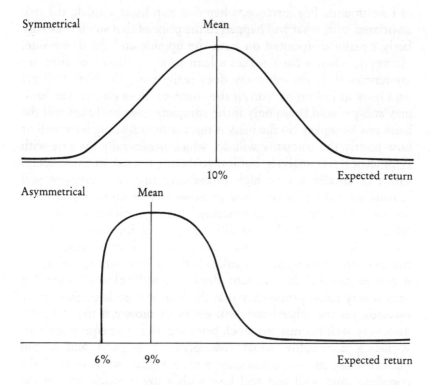

Figure 1.3   Risk distributions

you may be willing to accept a slightly lower expected return to prevent a major disaster.

Imagine the case of a portfolio manager. Most portfolio managers in the United States are evaluated in terms of how well they do against a certain benchmark. For stock portfolios this is usually the Standard and Poor's (S&P) 500. If someone told you that in good years, say when the market was up 20 percent, you would be up 17 percent, you might not be too happy. But if you were also told that in bad years, when the market was down 10 percent, your portfolio would only be down 2 percent, you might think that was pretty good. Portfolio managers are not usually fired for just barely underperforming the market. On the other hand, jobs can be lost if managers take big losses. So this type of insurance, where one buys protection against down-side risks and gives up a little bit of the up-side opportunity, is something that appeals to a number of portfolio managers.

One can see the asymmetry of risk in comparing different kinds of investments. For instance, when one purchases a stock, the risk associated with what will happen to the price of that stock is usually fairly equally distributed on both the up-side and the down-side. However, when a bank makes a loan to a company, the risks are asymmetrical. If the company does really well, the bank will get paid back in full on its loan; if the company does poorly, the bank may still get paid back; only if the company goes bankrupt will the bank not be repaid. So the bank is not really evaluating how well or how poorly the company will do, which is generally the case with symmetrical risk analysis, but it is analyzing the risk of bankruptcy. There is usually a very high probability that the company will remain solvent and a very low probability of bankruptcy risk. So the bank is seeing an asymmetrical risk distribution when it makes a loan, and as a result there is different pricing for loans compared with stock market values. Loans are priced with an interest rate. If the company does well, the bank gets the interest rate agreed upon; it gets no more if the company does *very* well; However, there is only a very small probability that the loan will go bad. The equity investor, on the other hand, will get more money if the company does very well because the stock price will rise. The equity investor is facing a roughly equal risk between a good and a bad performance; he will participate with a higher stock price if the company does well and will lose with a lower stock price if the company does poorly.

Another example of risk asymmetry is the mortgages that consumers take on when they buy a house. Virtually all mortgages in the United States have an option which allows the consumer to repay the original mortgage and refinance with a new mortgage and interest rate with virtually no penalty. This is known as the *refinance option* or no-prepayment penalty clause. When a bank makes a mortgage, it must somehow price the possibility that the consumer will refinance the mortgage if interest rates fall. That is, if a bank makes a loan at 14 percent for 30 years and interest rates fall to 10 percent over the next five years, the consumer may go back to the bank and say, 'I want a 10 percent mortgage rather than a 14 percent mortgage.' The bank, in the initial mortgage, has given the consumer the right to do just that. But that right has a price. The consumer has been given an option to refinance if interest rates fall, and he has paid for it with the up-front points or front-end fee on the mortgage as well as with the fact that mortgage interest rates exceed most other long-term rates. This is another example of risk asymmetry. It is asymmetric because if interest rates rise there is no way the consumer is going to refinance: he is going to stay with his 10 percent mortgage if interest rates go to 15 percent; he will refinance only if interest rates go lower, which is the one-sided part of it. It is an example of the premise that we always pay for risk, because the greater the probability that the refinancing option will be exercised, the more incentive the banks have to charge finance fees or points on the mortgage.

The primary new instrument on Wall Street that helps deal with the asymmetry of risk is *options*. Options give investors the ability to change the distribution of risk from symmetrical to asymmetrical or visa versa and as a result have become an extremely popular instrument on Wall Street. Options pricing is very complicated, but the important point here is that, as risks became greater in the 1970s and 1980s, investors and companies sought ways of managing risks. Options have the ability to actually change the risk distribution and have become a key tool. (Options are covered in detail in a later chapter.)

The lesson of this section is that it is not enough just to understand expected return and the risk involved in that return: one must also know something about the shape of the risk distribution. Is risk symmetric between the up-side and the down-side? If it is asymmetric, the pricing of the risk will be affected and may affect the instruments one chooses to manage risk.

Conclusions

In this chapter, the emphasis has been on identifying the basic concepts and providing some examples of how Wall Street applies these concepts to price risk against expected return. The implications of the analysis are three-fold. First, you pay for risks that cannot be avoided. Second, in portfolio analysis what matters is what the next investment does to the risk of the total portfolio. One evaluates not just the risk of a single investment, but how it affects the whole portfolio. This is the principle of portfolio diversification. Third, the shape of the risk distribution in terms of its up-side versus its down-side potential is an important element in the pricing of risk and an equally important element that must be considered in the construction of a portfolio of stocks.

These three principles of risk and return will be referred to time and time again as we go through the various markets. For instance, the tradeoffs between the stock and the bond markets, and the reason they sometimes move together and sometimes do not, will involve understanding how the risks and returns of stocks versus bonds are related. When we look at corporate finance issues later in the book we will be discussing such issues as the value to the stockholder when a corporation decides to diversify into other industries. Already hinted at, this may be a questionable strategy; for stockholders can already avoid some of these risks, and if they can already avoid the risk, they may not be willing to pay a higher stock price for the company to do it for them.

Finally, we will examine issues in interest rate risk management, comparing the use of financial futures and options. Options offer some useful advantages, not the least because they change the risk structure. Clearly, issues of risk and return will be a recurring theme of this book.

2

What You See May Not Be What You Get:
Expectations and Market Dynamics

Markets are forward-looking. As such, stock and bond prices reflect expectations of future events. To understand the critical tradeoffs between the risks and returns described in the preceding chapter, one must also understand how the market forms expectations about returns, and with what confidence those expectations are held. Thus, to understand why markets move the way they do, one must analyze what the market expects to happen in the future, why the market forms that expectation, what is likely to change it, and what risks are associated with those expectations. The answers to these questions provide significant insights into the dynamics of markets, such as why prices fall quickly or rise quickly under certain conditions and remain stable in others.

The study of market expectations has evolved around two very important concepts. The first is the concept of *market efficiency*, or how the market uses information. The second is the concept of *rational expectations*, which has to do with whether or not the expectations formed in the marketplace reflect the underlying structure of the economy.

In this chapter we will analyze these two concepts. The analysis will provide a basis for drawing certain conclusions about market dynamics. We will then combine the concepts of market efficiency and rational expectations with market dynamics to derive a set of implications that are applicable to both investment and corporate decision-making.

Basic Concepts

Market efficiency and rational expectations are two concepts developed by academic economists to describe how markets use information and form expectations about future events. These concepts are extremely critical because markets for stocks, bonds, foreign exchange, and all financial instruments are forward-looking. That is to say, the price of a stock reflects not so much the past achievements of the company as the market's confidence that those achievements can be extended into the future. In turn, the prices of bonds reflect market expectations about what inflation will be, what monetary policy will be, and what the future course of interest rates will be. Certainly, markets use history in forming expectations of future events; the concepts of market efficiency and rational expectations, however, go well beyond the use of historical perspective and attempt to describe how the market translates history into a forecast of future events.

Market efficiency describes how well the financial markets in their collective wisdom process information. An efficient market is defined as one in which all available information is utilized by the market to construct expectations of future events. This means that only surprises, or new information, can change the prices of securities. This is because the current price of a security has been determined by the market using all currently available information: the only information that is missing is future information. When that information is announced – whether it is in the form of government statistics, an earnings report by a company, or a change in policy by OPEC – prices will change if the new information is unexpected.

Not Everyone Has To Be a Lead Steer

There are varying degrees of market efficiency, but the concept does not require that every player in the market have access to all information. It requires only that key players in the market have access to available information, and that they buy and sell securities on that basis.

For example, there are some very large companies involved in the production, buying, and selling of wheat and grains around the world. These companies trade with each other in the cash and futures markets, and the result of the trades between them determines the world price for wheat. If you or I want to buy wheat on the Chicago Futures exchange, however, we can get exactly the same price that these very large, sophisticated companies get; yet we do not have to know anything about the economics of wheat production, the demand for wheat, and so forth. What has happened is that the very large sophisticated players in the market, by their competitive interaction, have processed information about the wheat market and its future prospects and have set a price for wheat. That price is available to all of us, whether or not we understand the economics of the wheat market.

One of my former colleagues, Joel Stern, refers to these price-setters as 'lead steers.' Lead steers may be the sophisticated portfolio managers on Wall Street; they may be individuals who manage trust or pension funds. There may very well be hundreds of lead steers – investors doing their homework, processing information, analyzing markets, and then buying or selling securities on that basis. The existence of a large group of sophisticated market players guarantees the efficiency of markets in a sense that information about companies and about the economy is processed very quickly and is immediately translated into the prices of stocks and bonds and other securities.

Insider Trading

The concept of market efficiency sometimes collides with an event known as 'insider trading.' Insiders are those executives of corporations or close associates who are privy to certain information that has not yet been made public. To the extent that these insiders have access to important information before it has become available to the market, they can take positions in securities to earn unusual profits.

The actual effect of insider trading on markets, however, is considerably less clear. Academic studies have been produced on both sides of the issue. One camp argues that insider information does not stay inside very long and that insiders have precious little time to take advantage of whatever information they may have. These academics suggest that insider trading is actually an insignificant problem. They cite statistical studies of the performance of corporate executives in terms of buying and selling their own stock and conclude that these insiders are not earning unusual profits.

Another camp notes a number of more spectacular cases of attempts to manipulate markets through insider information. They argue that, regardless of how profitable insider information may be on average, there is absolutely no question that certain individuals at certain times have attempted to make unusual profits from inside information.

The economic importance for markets is two-fold. First, it is not clear how much of a problem insider trading is because, if the insiders do any trading at all, the information antennae of the sophisticated investor community will pick this up and start to move on its own. The second point is a corollary to the first. The existence of insider trading may give a few individuals a very short lead on the market, but on average and over time, insider trading is not inconsistent with extremely efficient market behavior in terms of how expectations are processed and how prices of securities are set.

As a moral and legal issue, insider trading raises serious concerns. The United States Securities and Exchange Commission (SEC) has made the prosecution of insider trading a major focus of its regulatory process. The most spectacular abuses have occurred in the area of mergers and acquisitions (M&A).

If a Wall Street firm has a confidential relationship with a large industrial firm seeking to buy another firm, the insider information can be extremely valuable. Should a principal in the Wall Street firm handling the acquisition buy or sell securities based on that information, he would not only be guilty of violating the SEC insider trading regulations, but also might severely damage his firm's credibility as being capable of handling large transactions discreetly. In short, insider trading abuses can do serious harm to a firm's reputation, affecting its ability to attract M&A business in the future and, consequently, its future profitability. Such bottom-line consequences have resulted in increasingly strict procedures within Wall Street firms to police themselves and to prevent insider trading abuses.

In the international context, insider trading raises complex cross-culture issues. Certain markets, such as foreign exchange markets, do not have insider trading regulations; indeed, there are cases in which central banks are believed to have tipped off their local banks in advance of major changes in monetary policy that may affect foreign exchange rates. In the securities industry, practices differ around the world. What might be deemed insider trading by the SEC in the United States may be common business practice in Switzerland, for example, where brokers have always traded aggressively for their own accounts – along with those of their customers. In sum, there are a lot of grey areas involved in the insider trading controversy, and this is likely to remain the case for a very long time.

Expectations Are Often Wrong

Another issue that arises in the discussion of efficient markets is the question of how accurate market forecasts are of future events. On this question, the academic research is fairly conclusive. Market forecasts of future events are terrible.

For example, forward exchange rates, which allow investors to trade foreign exchange for three, six, or more months into the future based on prices set today, can be thought of as market forecasts of where investors think exchange rates will be three, six, or more months from today. These forecasts have historically been wrong – virtually always wrong.

The same thing has been true in other futures markets, whether one looks at commodities or financial instruments. For instance, you can buy wheat for delivery one year from now at a price set today. You can buy US Treasury bonds six months or a year from now at prices set today. The prices that are set today, for transactions that will take place some time in the future, contain explicit expectations of what future prices will be. And those expectations are consistently wrong.

This does not mean that the market is inefficient. The market may have done as good a job as possible in processing all available information, but as time passes new information becomes available, new events occur, and prices have to be reconsidered.

Expectations Are Not Biased

What *is* important is that market forecasts of future events are not biased consistently in one direction or another. That is, market forecasts of future prices are not continually overshooting or continually undershooting. If markets were always wrong by being 10 percent too high, then, once you and I figured that out, we could make a killing by beating the market out of that 10 percent every time. As a result, what happens in the market is that when there are streaks, times when the market misprices securities on either the up-side or the down-side for five or six months in a row, the market – analysts, investors, corporate executives – figures this out, and actions are taken by investors in terms of buying and selling securities that eliminate the bias.

The concept of market efficiency argues that expectations of future events should be unbiased, but it does not argue that they should be accurate. For the most part, the statistical research done on this issue tends to confirm that, while market expectations of future events can run in streaks during which there are significant periods when the market over- or underestimates future prices, over long periods of time the market is an unbiased forecaster – even if it is a very bad forecaster.

Are Markets a Random Walk?

The last issue raised by market efficiency is one that has become known in the stock market literature as the theory of the *random walk*. The argument goes like this. The market has already processed all available information into the prices of securities, and only surprises can change the price of securities in the future. Surprises, by definition, are not known today. Furthermore, surprises are thought to occur at random, because if they did not occur at random they would not be surprises. So, following this line of reasoning, the only way one can beat the market, in the sense of buying undervalued stocks that will rise in price in the future, is to be lucky. The market is a 'random walk.'

Now, if the market is a random walk, an optimal investment strategy would not be to try to beat the market, since this may not be possible except with luck. Consequently, those believing in the theory of the random walk are strong advocates of the investment strategy known as *indexation*. As mentioned earlier, indexation is when one buys the whole market or an index of the market. The portfolio is constructed such that, if stock prices rise 10 percent on average, the portfolio will be up 10 percent. Such a portfolio trys only to track the market as a whole and not to beat the market.

The random walk theory has a lot to commend it. But there is a key question that is not answered by the theory: Who keeps the market honest? Who is processing all the information that makes the market efficient, and how are those people rewarded?

Processing information and then turning it into a decision to buy or sell stocks is costly. It takes time to analyze information – and time is money. Sophisticated corporations, investors, and fund managers spend a lot of time processing information about the economy and translating it into a portfolio strategy. These people make the market efficient, but in doing so they have to be rewarded. And they have to be rewarded relative to the risk they are assuming in attempting the difficult job of analyzing markets and trying to beat those markets. In this context, it should not be surprising that some pension fund managers, portfolio managers, foreign exchange traders, and bond traders – or some other set of sophisticated investors – can in fact, beat the market on average and over time.

By how much can they beat the market? The average earnings of this group of superior investors are thought to be quite large. But by the same token, the risks that they assume are also thought to be large and their income streams highly variable. In this context, they probably are being fairly rewarded for what they do for society, namely, the efficient processing of information. These people are not necessarily making excessive profits, because they are in a difficult and risky profession.

In any case, the debate on whether or not one can beat the market is likely to go on for quite some time. The view of efficient markets that has been discussed here strongly suggests that markets price information very quickly, and that, while beating the market may be possible, it is a risky, full-time occupation.

Rational Expectations

Associated with the concept of market efficiency is one of rational expectations. The idea behind this concept is that expectations are formed by the market in a way that is consistent with the actual economic structure of the market. What this means is that, if the monetarists are right and money supply growth eventually leads to inflation, then market expectations of future inflation will reflect, over time and on average, the information known about the growth of the money supply.

Just as with the concept of efficient markets, the concept of rational expectations does not require every investor to see the world the same way; nor does it require every investor to be an expert in economics. It only requires that the prices that result in the marketplace be some average of all investors' expectations, and that the average price reflect the underlying market structure.

A particular person may have a great deal of athletic talent, and yet, if you asked him to explain how he achieved success in his particular sport, he might not be able to explain the physics of that sport. The same thing can be true in markets. Corporate executives may be very good at running their company but very poor at explaining the economics of how markets really work, even in the industry in which they themselves are involved. But they have developed rules of thumb – intuition – that have made them good at their jobs.

The theory of rational expectations is consistent with the concept discussed earlier, that market forecasts are very poor but they are unbiased. Rational expectations does not in any way suggest that the market has an unusual capability to forecast accurately. We know there are many surprise events that occur, and that these can change the price behavior of securities. The discussion here, and the point to be made, is the same as with efficient markets: if the market were consistently biased in one direction or another in forming expectations there would be an exploitable opportunity for the investor community, and as it was exploited, the bias would disappear.

Technical Analysis and Market Structure

The importance of rational expectations is that it suggests that market expectations, in their collective sense, reflect the underlying structure of the market. Expectations are not simply an extrapolation of history. They are formed by a much more complex process, which makes an attempt to understand why the history occurred the way it did.

In this regard, the concepts of efficient markets and rational expectations run headlong into a market forecasting technique known as *technical analysis*. Technical analysis is a code word for the process of looking at charts of past patterns of price movements and deriving implications for future movements on that basis alone. From the point of view of an economist, technical analysis is like driving a car backwards looking only through the rear view mirror. You do fine along the straight, both uphill and downhill, but the hairpin turns are going to nail you every time. Rational expectations, in its view that in some way the market has an understanding of economic structure, is important in steering the investor around these hairpin turns because some of the most critical changes in the prices of securities have to do with changes in market structure.

One example is the deregulation of the financial community in 1980, which had a very important and direct impact on the stock prices of banks, insurance companies, and brokerage houses as well as on the formation of monetary policy. This is just one illustration of how a change in market structure affected the pattern of securities prices. Changes in the tax structure are another. By altering taxes, the government can provide incentives to invest, or they can discourage investors. This changes the fortunes of companies, and it changes the way security prices move. These are issues of market structure. And the theory of rational expectations suggests that market expectations are formed with a great deal more knowledge than of just where prices have been in the past.

Implications

The combination of these two concepts of efficient markets and rational expectations argues that the market uses all available information, and that, in the market's collective wisdom, this includes an understanding of the structure of the economy. Neither of these concepts requires everyone (or even anyone) in the market to possess all information or to understand exactly how the economy works. They only argue that the market collectively, by different investors with different ideas, buying and selling securities in a competitive marketplace, decides what the prices will be.

These theories do not imply that one cannot beat the market, because there must be a role for the information processors to earn their living – the ones who actually keep the market honest and make it efficient and rational. But it does suggest that the profession of keeping the market honest is a risky one, and that it will earn high rewards relative to these high risks but that those rewards will not be excessive relative to the risks taken.

Furthermore, these theories do not suggest that market forecasts are accurate. In fact, these theories are consistent with very wrong market forecasts, just so long as the forecasts are not consistently wrong in one direction. Market efficiency and rational expectations argue that market forecasts are unbiased but not acccurate.

Market Dynamics

Market expectations and their formation have a great deal to do with the speed at which prices move in the market. These dynamics are extremely tricky. All that the concepts of rational expectations and market efficiency tell us about market dynamics is that information is processed quickly and in some relationship to the underlying economic structure. That is not very much information to go on.

Discounting the Future

The critical judgement to be made when analyzing market behavior is on what the market is expecting and why. In stock market language, this is called knowing what has been 'discounted' by the market.

For example, if it is widely believed that the Federal Reserve is likely to cut the *discount rate* over the next several weeks, then bond prices will reflect that belief. When the discount rate is actually cut, bond prices may not move very much, because the expectation that was discounted into the market was realized. On the other hand, if for some reason the Federal Reserve chooses not to cut the discount rate, when everyone thought it was going to, then bond prices may react quite negatively, because the expectation of a discount rate cut proved to be incorrect.

What this example shows is the important function that expectations play in the timing of a price movement. Major events that are widely anticipated may have absolutely no effect on prices at the time they occur. Other, equally major, events can have profound impacts on prices if they were not anticipated. The first lesson, then, of market dynamics and expectations is that one must know what future events have already been discounted by the market.

Credibility

In terms of announcements that governments may make about future policies or that corporations may make about their future earnings capability, there is an additional consideration, which is the credibility of the announcement. A leading politician may announce that the US Congress is going to enact a tax cut or cut the budget deficit or perform some other major act, but this may have absolutely no market impact because the announcement has no credibility. By the same token, the executive of a corporation may announce that next year's earnings are going to be up 50 percent but if he has been saying the same thing for the last four years and earnings have been flat, his current announcement will have no effect on the stock price.

On the other hand, when the announcement is credible the effect can be significant and immediate. When Paul Volcker, as Chairman of the Federal Reserve Board, announced in October 1979 that he was tightening US monetary policy to reduce inflation and support the value of the dollar, interest rates went up immediately – not just because the Federal Reserve said it was tightening policy, but because the market believed that the Federal Reserve was serious about what it said it was going to do.

The credibility of policy announcements has caused a great deal of trouble for politicians. When President Reagan went into office in 1981, many of his advisors argued that his tax cut proposals would result in an almost immediate improvement in the economy, because people would believe his promise and would begin to act on their belief immediately. What, in fact, occurred was a great deal of cynicism about the pronouncement. Because previous governments had not been credible in their pronouncements of policy, the market was not sure that the tax cuts would be made, or how they would be structured. Consequently, the economic boom that was forecast did not occur in 1981 or 1982 but arrived only after the tax cuts were actually enacted, in 1983 and 1984.

Another important consideration in the interaction between market dynamics and expectations is how financial markets react to the flood of economic statistics provided by the US government about the US economy. In the last several years, market reactions to releases of economic data have been quite swift and sometimes even violent, only to be reversed in a few weeks as other pieces of data are released. Indeed, the sensitivity of interest rates and stock prices to the release of economic data is an incredible phenomenon. It is incredible because most of the data are eventually revised, many of them are conflicting, and it takes a long time to put together a reasonable picture of what is happening to the economy. But the costs of missing the next move in stock prices or interest rates have become so large that even one more piece of information has taken on added importance.

This can been seen quite clearly in the market's attention on Thursday afternoons at 4:30 p.m. when the Federal Reserve releases its banking statistics for the week. The Federal Reserve makes a point of being very secretive in its policy deliberations, but because it is such an important institution and plays such a key role in the future direction of interest rates, the market cannot wait for the 'Fed' to reveal what it is planning to do: the market has to try to figure it out. These weekly data releases sometimes provide the best clues as to what the Fed is trying to do. As a result, a great deal of attention is placed on these data releases, and many times the market gets it wrong. It misreads the clues. However, the fact that the market gets it wrong many times does not mean that one can avoid looking at the numbers that come out on Thursday afternoon. Occasionally they contain clear and important clues.

One of the important roles that economists play on the analysis teams of portfolio managers, corporations, and so forth is providing a judgement on how new economic data fit into the whole picture as it is currently evolving. This service occasionally leads to good forecasts, and can often lead to bad forecasts, but is nonetheless a critical part of analyzing new economic data. This process is part and parcel of why the markets are efficient and why expectations are formed rationally.

Strategic Implications

These discussions of market efficiency, rational expectations, and the dynamics of markets have highlighted a number of issues in the pricing of securities. It is all well and good to understand the tradeoffs in risk and return, but, equally important, one must understand why the expected return is what it is and why the risk assessment is what it is. In short, it is the expectations process that sets the risk and the returns that investors trade off against each other.

Some of the implications from this view of market expectations and market dynamics can be summarized. First, a premium is put on credibility by those that make announcements to the market. Corporate spokesmen announcing the future earnings potential of a company must have credibility if those announcements are to translate into higher stock prices. Similarly, government spokesmen must have credibility if the market is to give credit today for what the government may do in the future. This has implications for how a corporation should run its investor relations department; it must give the market the information it needs relative to the understanding of how that industry is structured, and it must provide information that is credible.

A second lesson is that investors, as well as corporate managers, must know the market. They must understand which expectations are built into the market and why. Knowing what has been built into the market helps one analyze market movements when those expectations are not satisfied. Knowing why those expectations are in the market helps one analyze how those expectations will change as future economic data are released or government announcements on policy are made.

A final point is that, while it may not be impossible for a portfolio manager to outperform the market, his is a full-time job with a lot of risk, and a portfolio manager who can consistently beat the market should be well paid. In a sense, these types of people are the lead steers – the information processors who keep the market honest and make it efficient.

Part II
Equity Markets

3

What's It Worth To You?
How Wall Street Values a Company

The price at which the shares of a company trade on the open market determines the value of the company. This price is set by the interaction of a multitude of buyers and sellers who determine the supply and demand for the shares.

This chapter takes a fundamental view of how these share prices are determined. There are some who argue that the market responds to psychological impulses – that investors join bandwagons and push stock prices to levels that are too high or too low in terms of fundamental value. There exists, however, a significant number of academic studies, as well as market research reports compiled by sophisticated investor organizations, which strongly suggest that key fundamental factors play an extremely important role in the determination of share prices.

To examine the fundamental determinants of share prices, the first step will be to take a top-down approach, starting with the effects of the overall economy, the industry, and the quality of management. This will be followed by a bottoms-up approach, which focuses on the operational characteristics of a firm, its capital structure, and its ability to innovate. These methods for analyzing share prices are mutually consistent and provide useful insights in terms of investment strategy and corporate financial management.

A Macroeconomic Perspective

From a macroeconomic perspective, share prices are influenced by three broad factors: (1) the general performance of the economy, including changes in interest rates, inflation, and real economic growth; (2) the performance of a given industry; and (3) the quality of management within a specific firm. Roughly speaking, economic factors probably account for about one-quarter of the movement in a given share's price. Industry factors probably account for roughly another one-quarter, and the quality of management accounts for the rest. This implies that, even if a firm had the best possible management team in place, the team's efforts would determine only about half of the company's value. The other half would be determined by forces beyond the control of any management team – the industry's performance, and various economic variables such as interest rates, inflation, or real economic activity.

The Economy

The first factor to examine is the general economic performance of the whole country, and in a sense the whole world, since many of the corporations we are dealing with are multinational in nature. Three key economic variables are real economic growth, inflation, and interest rates. For the most part, corporate profits will expand when real economic growth is strong.

The effect of inflation on corporate profits, however, is unclear. Many corporate assets such as equipment and buildings will actually appreciate in value during inflationary times, and the corporation, depending on the competitiveness of its industry, may well be able to pass on cost increases in the form of price increases. So, whether inflation is a positive or a negative factor on the value of a corporation will depend on the industry and a variety of competitive factors.

The last economic factor is interest rates, which tend to have negative effects since higher interest rates are associated with lower corporate profitability and lower corporate values. The relationship between interest rates and the stock market, however, is extremely complicated. In the microeconomic perspective of the value of the firm, which will be discussed in the next section of this chapter, this issue will come in for considerable discussion. Also, chapter 10 is devoted entirely to the relationship between interest rates and the stock market. For now, the primary point is that higher interest rates are generally bad for the stock market and bad for individual firms, while lower interest rates are a positive factor.

Industry Factors

Industry factors are as important as general economic factors in the determination of share prices. These factors include the level of competition within the industry and the performance of the industry in question relative to other industries. In terms of competition, the closer an industry is to a monopoly, the more likely it is that cost increases can be passed on to consumers in the form of price increases. Furthermore, in a non-competitive environment, profitability tends to be higher.

Competition, however, is not easy to assess. A number of industries have very high capital requirements which make it difficult for new firms to enter the market in a short period of time. However, if excess profits are earned in this industry over a long period of time owing to a lack of competitition, very large firms in other industries will be likely to make those substantial capital expenditures, enter the market, and eventually make this particular industry more competitive.

An extreme example of this was provided by the behavior of the Organization of Petroleum Exporting Countries (OPEC) in the 1970s. In the early 1970s OPEC controlled over 40 percent of the oil market and, using that leverage, drove prices up to extremely high levels in 1974 and again in 1979. The initial effect of these price increases was to expand dramatically OPEC profits.

The decade-long effect was two-fold. First, many conservation practices were put in place which decreased the long-term demand for oil and other energy-related products. And second, many new sources of supply entered the market. The North Sea, which at oil prices below $10 a barrel was not considered profitable, became an extremely profitable place to explore for oil when it was priced above $30 a barrel. Many other areas in which oil was known to exist but was costly to extract were also developed in the late 1970s. The resulting increase in oil supplied from non-OPEC sources cut OPEC's market share nearly in half and turned a monopoly-type market into a fully competitive one. Thus, it is important when analyzing industry factors to take both a short-term view of the competitive nature of the industry and a long-term view.

Another factor affecting the competitiveness of an industry is its regulatory environment. In a number of industries, the government has tended to protect producers. In the United States this is particularly true in the area of utilities, with the production and distribution of electricity as a prime example. Telecommunications is another industry that is highly regulated around the world and, as a result, has tended to earn monopoly profits.

The critical factor for assessing the impact on share prices is to observe what happens when the regulatory environment changes. There have been numerous examples over the last ten years because of significant deregulation. A classic example in the United States is the airline industry. Prior to deregulation, airline routes were tightly regulated by the US government in a manner that virtually guaranteed airlines substantial profits. High prices dominated because entry into the market was limited by the government. As the government withdrew from regulating market entry, many new airlines offering cheap fares entered the industry. Now it is not uncommon for a multitude of airlines to compete on what used to be highly profitable routes but are now high-volume, low-profit routes. Furthermore, entry by a large number of new cut-rate firms has so raised the level of competition that there are probably too many firms in the industry for the given level of traffic. As a consequence, a number of airlines have gone bankrupt and there are some more that are close to bankruptcy.

Thus, the change of a regulatory stucture from a protective status which allows excessive profits to a competitive status will generally reduce the profitability of the industry and put a premium on the final factor to be discussed, the quality of management.

Quality of Management

The quality of management in this top-down approach to the determination of share prices explains about half of the value of a company. Management quality takes many different forms and is extremely difficult to identify. Essentially, it is exemplified by the consistency of a firm's earnings and its ability to innovate and develop new products to earn high returns in the future.

The many different approaches to management quality are well beyond the scope of this book, but one area *is* within the realm of the current discussion and that is management compensation. Like everyone else, corporate management can be expected to respond to incentives. In this regard, the executive compensation schemes of corporations can be extremely important in determining the long-run consistency of a firm's management and earnings capability.

The critical variable to watch and analyze is whether the compensation scheme links up the interest of management with the interest of shareholders. That is to say, if management is expected to maximize the value of the firm, then the executive compensation scheme should provide incentives for attaining that goal.

Certain management compensation schemes may be based on an

accounting framework that does not accurately reflect how the fundamental value of a firm is determined in the market. These compensation schemes may lead to improper incentives which put shareholders at odds with management. This issue will resurface again in chapter 5 on the economics of the corporate accounting framework.

The point here, however, is two-fold. First, even the very best management is going to affect only about half the value of the company. (As we have seen, the other half is related to economic and industry conditions.) Second, the compensation scheme under which management operates is a critical factor because it determines whether shareholder interests and management interests are similar or are opposed to each other. Obviously, the latter situation can be detrimental to a firm's share price. The key example of this is a hostile takeover situation in which shareholders are offered a significant premium over the stock's current value on Wall Street yet management resists because they do not want to lose their jobs.

A Microeconomic Perspective

In terms of a microeconomic perspective on how Wall Street sets share prices, there are three broad categories for discussion. First, one must analyze the operating characteristics of the firm: that is, what is the firm's ability to generate cash flow? This operating cash flow must be considered on an after-tax basis and before any financing charges. The second broad category is the capital structure of the firm. It is within this topic that the financing of the firm is evaluated as well as the firm's utilization of available tax incentives such as the deductibility of interest. The third category is the firm's ability to innovate. Future earnings capabilities will depend in part on the success of investment activity undertaken today. The ability of management to identify high-return investments and to position the company to take advantage of those investments is a major factor in any firm's long-term success. These three categories – operating cash flow, capital structure, and investment activity – form the framework for determining the value of a corporation and the value of its shares.

Operating Cash Flow

The ability of a firm to produce a consistent and positive cash flow from its basic operations is obviously a critical factor. In evaluating a firm, one must assess future prospects for this stream of cash and then discount this stream of cash, assigning it a value today.

The cash flow that is being discussed here, however, is not the one that is generally reported in corporate earnings statements. We are interested not so much in today's earnings as in future earnings. Furthermore, it is important to separate the effect of taxes and financial structure from the earnings stream. There is a whole variety of ways in which a firm can be financed, and each method has different costs and different tax implications. In analyzing a firm it is important to separate the on-going business of the firm – its operating cash flow – from its financial structure. These are separate decisions. Therefore, when looking at operating cash flow, it should be observed on an after-tax basis and before interest expense.

The confidence that one has in a firm's ability to generate positive future cash flows depends on one's subjective assessment of the quality of management. Certainly, the ability of a given management team to produce consistent cash flows in the past is an excellent sign. Once an estimate of future operating cash flows, after taxes and before interest expense, has been determined, it must be given a present value. This is accomplished through the use of an interest rate that we call the *cost of capital*.

The cost of capital is essentially the sum of a risk-free interest rate, such as a US Treasury bond yield, plus a risk premium, reflecting conditions in the industry, in the economy, and in the management of a firm. The construction of a cost of capital for an individual firm is a fairly complex task and utilizes a concept known as *beta*, which measures the volatility of a firm's share price relative to the market as a whole. The next chapter discusses these aspects of beta in detail. For now, one need only realize that the cost of capital includes some measure of the riskiness of the firm and the industry in which it operates. Utilizing this cost of capital as an interest rate, one can discount a future stream of earnings and assign it a present value.

Capital Structure

The second issue in this bottoms-up approach to analyzing the value of a firm is the capital structure question. How does a firm finance itself?

There are several issues involved, but the most important one has to do with the tax structure. In the United States, as in many countries, interest on debt is tax-deductible. As a result, this makes debt financing attractive relative to equity financing. A corporation's use of debt relative to equity will be determined in part by the advantages of the tax deductibility of interest relative to the increased financial risk that a firm assumes by moving to a more highly leveraged status, that is, a higher debt/equity ratio. In general, a firm will have a higher overall value if it is more highly leveraged, unless the increased leverage subjects the firm to too much financial risk. That is, at higher leverage ratios, changes in market interest rates that are out of management's control and are often difficult to predict can dramatically affect the firms ability to stay in business.

There are many analysts who believe that no firm should have a triple-A credit rating because this indicates a failure to take even conservative advantage of the tax deductibility of interest on debt. On the other hand, it may not be prudent to go all the way to a triple-Z rating, because this would greatly increase the probability of bankruptcy and would reduce the value of the firm. The appropriate credit rating of the firm and its leverage ratio will depend on the competitiveness of the industry and the correlation between the firm's business, its operating plan, and what happens to interest rates. Some would argue that credit ratings between triple-B and single-A are appropriate for a great many firms.

Investment and Innovation

The final factor is the firm's ability to innovate. This addresses the issue of whether the company can successfully invest for the future.

There is probably a finite number of investment projects that can be expected to earn relatively high rates of return. As illustrated in figure 3.1, as new projects are considered, the expected returns decline — an example of the *law of diminishing returns.* The horizontal line running across the graph represents the firm's *cost of capital.* Generally speaking, new projects that can be expected to earn a return above the firm's cost of capital, sometimes known as the firm's *hurdle rate,* will add value to the firm. Projects that are expected to earn a positive return but less than the cost of capital will not add value to the firm and will not increase a firm's share price.

This is a simple axiom of alternative investments. The cost of capital in some sense represents an alternative use of funds. That is, the firm could invest money in similar firms in its own or other

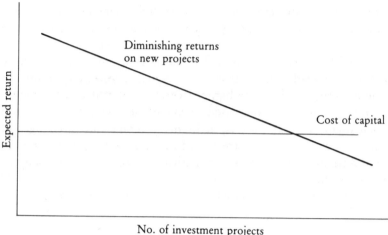

Figure 3.1   Investment projects and the cost of capital

industries and expect to earn a return equal to or above the risk-adjusted cost of capital. So, if an equal or higher risk-adjusted return can be earned in other investments, it would not make sense to pursue a project that could not at least match the cost of capital.

The confidence that investors have in management's ability to innovate – to invest successfully for the future – is a critical, subjective part of the determination of share prices. There is no rule of thumb. Quite obviously, this involves Wall Street's general assessment of the quality of management.

What Management Controls

In summary, as we look back over these three characteristics – operating cash flow, capital structure, and investment strategy – we see that management quality is the key variable in determining a firm's operating ability, in setting its capital structure appropriately to take advantage of the tax structure, and in determining which investment projects should be undertaken to enhance the future value of the firm. But one may also note that the cost of capital depends primarily on the level of interest rates in the economy, the determination of which is outside management's control. This cost of capital is used to value operating cash flows and as a hurdle rate, and determines which investments the firm should undertake. So one very important variable – the cost of capital – is outside the control of management and will vary with interest rates, and to a lesser extent with changing conditions in the industry.

Also outside the control of management is the tax structure. Most governments regularly make changes in their tax structure. These changes will affect the firms' value, their investment strategies, and perhaps even their basic operational plans. Management must be good at adapting to these changes, but it cannot control them.

From this bottoms-up approach, one can see then that, while management makes a major contribution to the determination of the value of the firm, there are key variables that lie outside management's control. Industry and general economic conditions have an equally important say.

Price/Earnings Ratios

This analysis of how a firm's fundamental value is determined by Wall Street has not yet referred to *price/earnings ratios*. The price/earnings (PE) ratio is common shorthand used by the market to describe how the price of a stock compares with its earnings stream. Price/earnings ratios for firms within a given industry and across industries can be quite different. These differences arise because firms within a given industry may utilize a different capital structure; or they may not have a quality of management that gives the market confidence in their ability to construct an appropriate investment strategy.

Changes in PE ratios are very important as a shorthand for following what has happened in the market, even though the ratios themselves are flawed in some very important ways. These flaws have to do with the difference between fundamental economics and accounting structure. A number of accounting conventions are useful for tax purposes but misrepresent the true value of a firm. This is a critical topic which is tackled in chapter 6.

PE ratios are also affected by the general move of interest rates. Generally speaking, the ratios will rise as interest rates fall. This occurs because, as interest rates fall, the cost of capital is reduced. This raises the present value of any earnings stream and will raise the price/earnings ratio.

It is important to remember that the PE ratio is just a quick shorthand for how a firm and its share price are doing. While it is often useful, it can occasionally be misleading.

Conclusion and Applications

There are many who say that the stock market follows psychological patterns. It gets on bandwagons and overvalues and then undervalues certain stocks. The view taken here is that the market (meaning Wall Street) is not capricious, but in its collective wisdom produces an evaluation of a corporation that has a strong relationship to fundamental economic theory.

From a top-down approach, this theory suggests that economic and industry conditions probably determine about half the changes in share prices and the ability of management determines the other half. From a bottoms-up approach, management is clearly the determining factor in a firm's operating cash flow, capital structure, and investment strategy. But in the calculation of these factors, one must utilize interest rates, which are market-determined, and a tax structure, which is government-determined. Both of these factors are of critical importance and lie well outside the control of management.

Also in terms of the bottoms-up approach, an analysis of the firm should separate operating characteristics from financial characteristics: first see if the operation is sufficiently profitable, and then decide how to finance it.

Finally, corporate investment strategies must be evaluated not in terms of whether they earn a positive return, but in terms of whether that positive return exceeds a firm's cost of capital. If I can earn 10 percent in one market and 5 percent in another, I would be a fool not to take the 10 percent if the risks were equal. That is the role that the cost of capital plays in determing which investment projects a firm should accept. It is in fact the hurdle rate over which investment projects must jump if they are to add value to a firm.

A final, classic, example of this last point closes this chapter and comes in the area of divestiture. Some firms have gotten into investment projects which clearly are not working, but they continue to pour capital into them. That is, they spend more and more investment funds on projects that are not likely to earn high returns. When a firm retreats from one of these businesses, its stock price may actually rise because it is no longer throwing good money after bad. On the day Texas Instruments announced that it was abandoning the personal computer business, the stock went from about $100 per share to over $120 per share. This 20 percent increase in the value of the stock came at a time when the company announced that it was taking a huge write-off and losing a lot of money, but leaving an unprofitable business behind. In short, once the stock market found out that Texas Instruments was no longer going to throw any more money at these unprofitable projects, it increased its valuation of the company.

4

Betas and Bets:
The Cost of Capital

The cost of capital is a critical concept in the analysis of how firms finance their operations and their investment projects. In essence, the cost of capital represents a risk-adjusted interest rate which is used to compute the present value of the cash flows from operations and which serves as a hurdle rate for evaluating investment projects. This concept is closely linked to the concept of beta, introduced first in chapter 1, in discussing the economics of risk and return, and used again in chapter 3, when examining how Wall Street values firms.

The purpose here is to link the investment decisions that individuals and portfolio managers make with the decisions of corporate executives. Conceptually, an important bridge between the investor and the corporation is the cost of capital and beta.

In this chapter, we will first review the concept of beta from the perspective of the investor. Then we will look at the corporate concept of the cost of capital. Finally, we will explicitly link the two concepts by showing how beta can be used to calculate a firm's cost of capital.

Beta: An Investor Perspective

For the investor, deciding which equities to purchase when putting together a portfolio of common stocks is a little like shopping in the supermarket of risk and return. For the risk-averse, there is the aisle containing the non-nuclear utilities. (The nuclear-powered utilities are over in a riskier aisle.) The food retailers are not too risky, and are close to the non-nuclear utilities. For the risk-takers, the airline stocks and the high-technology companies are on the far side of the store, in the risky aisles. These riskier aisles are cheaper, meaning they offer the potential for higher returns.

The measure developed by academic research and adopted by Wall Street to summarize certain risk characteristics of a stock is known as *beta*. And the aisles of the supermarket of risk and return are designated by different betas.

The concept of beta was derived by observing the behavior of stocks over both boom and bust periods. One quickly notices that certain groups of stocks seem to outperform the general market in good times, and to lead the market down in bad times. That is, these stocks swing with the market, but magnify its movements.

Other groups of stocks move with the market, but seem to dampen its moves. As the stock market booms, these stocks move up, but not by as much. Conversely, when the market in general is in a bust cycle, these stocks decline in price, but only modestly.

As was discussed in chapter 2 on risk and return, beta measures how a given stock or a portfolio of stocks moves with the total market for all common stocks. For standardization, the entire market has a beta of 1.00. Stocks that magnify general market moves have betas that are greater than 1, such as the airline industry at around 1.5. Stocks that dampen market moves and are less volatile are assigned betas less than 1, such as food retailers at around 0.8.

Over time and on average, there is a strong relationship between the beta of a particular stock or portfolio and the total return received from holding that stock relative to the whole market. Using 60 years of data, researchers have produced estimates of the return differentials that are potentially available from taking on more risk, as defined by holding a portfolio of stocks with relatively high betas. These returns have been quantified in real terms, that is, after adjusting for inflation over the years.

The results indicate that a very low beta portfolio, say, one consisting solely of US Treasury bills of very short-term maturities, will yield, over time and on average, no more than the inflation rate. In real terms, this is an expected return of 0. On the other hand, this portfolio has excellent capital preservation characteristics. Since one never takes capital losses, the only risk faced is keeping up with inflation, and research supports the notion that the returns from this portfolio will just equal the inflation rate.

By contrast, a portfolio of common stocks, with a beta of 1.0, over time and on average, will do very nicely. The returns received from taking the additional risk of capital losses result in significantly higher average returns over long time periods. In this case, the returns exceeded the inflation rate by almost 6 percent, indicating a real return of that magnitude.

This is not the end of the story. By taking even more risk, such as investing totally in a portfolio of small-capitalization growth stocks, the potential returns available over long time periods are extremely high. Unfortunately, during shorter time periods substantial losses are possible. The good times, however, far exceed the bad times, and for investors with staying power, potential returns of 8.8 percent over and above inflation were realized during the research period.

The results for these three portfolios are summarized in Table 4.1. This is a real-world representation of the risk and return concepts discussed in detail in chapter 1. These concepts drive Wall Street, because of the large differences in return available for taking additional risks.

Table 4.1   Historical average returns, 1926–1981

Portfolio	(1) Inflation-adjusted average return (%)	(2) Nominal average return (%)	(3) St. dev. of nominal returns (%)
Treasury bills	0.0	3.0	3.1
Common stocks	5.9	9.1	21.9
Small stocks	8.8	12.1	37.3

Note: The nominal average return presented in col. (2) measures the actual returns earned over the entire period and presented as an annual average. The standard deviations of these returns presented in col. (3), provide a measure of the variability of the returns, with the 37.3% for common stocks indicating a more more volatile pattern of earnings over the entire period than the 3.1% standard deviation for the Treasury bill portfolio.

Source: Roger G. Ibbotson and Rex A. Sinquefield, *Stocks, Bonds, Bills and Inflation*, Financial Analysts Research Foundation, Charlottesville, Virginia, 1982.

The Corporate Uses of Beta

The concept of beta is clearly useful for investors involved in structuring a portfolio. The investors' use of beta revolves directly around the risk and return tradeoffs offered by the market.

Investors seeking higher returns must take more risk, and beta is a useful guide to that additional risk.

This also means that investors' willingness to supply capital to the stock market, used to fund the new projects of corporations, depends on risk and return tradeoffs and is related to the concept of beta. Whether a stock's price will go up or down as new investment opportunities are undertaken will depend very much on the prospective returns of these projects relative to the risks being taken. Corporations will be making this assessment, but so, of course, will investors.

In this sense, corporations can be viewed as investors when they are deciding which new ventures to undertake. The economic costs of new ventures will bear a strong relationship to their riskiness.

For the corporation, the concept that embodies a measure of risk in determining a firm's financing costs is the cost of capital. The rule of thumb is quite clear. New projects that offer prospective returns exceeding their cost of capital are likely to enhance the value of a company and raise its share price. The application of this rule is anything but clear. Problems lie in the areas of making judgements on a project's prospective returns and in measuring the true cost of capital, among others. The reader interested in the serious technicalities of these issues must be prepared to wade through textbooks in corporate finance. In this chapter, we only want to highlight one very key issue.

Borrowing Costs versus the Cost of Capital

There is a world of difference between accounting returns and economic returns. Stock market valuation depends on economic returns. In the next chapter this topic is covered in detail, but one important application is in the area of the cost of capital.

Once a firm has decided to undertake a new investment project, it must decide how to finance the project. There are several choices, but only two are discussed here: to borrow the money from the bond market, or to attract new funds by issuing new shares of stock. That is, we are going to compare the stock market to the bond market as sources of funds for the new project.

If a firm chooses to issue bonds, then it will have to pay an interest rate that reflects the firm's credit rating. Provided that the bond issue is not so large in itself to cause a change in the firm's bond rating, the interest rate at which the firm can borrow can be assessed with no difficulty. In general, the interest rate on the new bonds will be virtually the same as the current yields on the firm's already outstanding bonds.

For example purposes, say this firm can borrow at 10 percent. What matters to the firm is the after-tax cost of borrowing. If this is a profitable, tax-paying firm in the 34 percent tax bracket, then the cost of borrowing is not the 10 percent interest rate, but actually 6.6 percent. (This is calculated as 1 minus the tax rate times the market interest rate.)

From this calculation of the firm's after-tax, 6.6 percent borrowing cost, the firm might be tempted to undertake all projects that offered returns exceeding 6.6 percent. Such projects, indeed, would add to the firm's after-tax income on an accounting basis. Unfortunately, the stock market may see things differently. The stock price may not rise, if the increase in earnings from the new ventures are not deemed worthy of the risks being taken.

The key is that the after-tax borrowing cost is not the cost of capital. The bond market is concerned only with the risk of the firm going bankrupt, not with the returns that may or may not be available from new projects, since bond investors will not participate in those gains if they occur.

The stock market on the other hand, is vitally concerned with the potential profitability of new projects, regardless of how they are financed. Furthermore, the stock market assesses the risk associated with any new investment projects a firm may undertake. New projects that are to add value for stock market investors must meet a much tougher standard than the bond market applies. All the bond market needs to know is that the new projects will not contribute to the risk that the firm will go bankrupt. The stock market, however, makes its judgements on whether the risk-adjusted expected returns from the new projects exceed the current risk–adjusted returns which are expected of the firm by the market. In other words, stock market investors require new project returns to exceed a risk-adjusted cost of capital for the project.

The cost of capital is always higher than a firm's after-tax cost of borrowing. Thus, there often exist investment projects offering returns that exceed the after-tax cost of borrowing but are less than the cost of capital. These projects will return an accounting profit and add after-tax income to the bottom line. Unfortunately, they will detract from a company's share price. The reason is that on a risk-adjusted basis the project does not offer returns equal to those available on other similarly risky projects. In short, investors have better things to do with their money than to give it to corporations, only to have the corporations invest in projects that offer lower returns than alternative investments available to stockholders.

This principal is illustrated in figure 4.1, and it is the same one discussed in the previous chapter. As we may recall, the downward-sloping line describes investment projects available to a firm, where the expected return on each succeeding project is less than the last. This just indicates that it gets harder and harder to find high-return projects. In economics, this is known as the *law of diminishing returns.*

The two horizontal lines represent the cost of capital and the after-tax borrowing cost, respectively. As can be seen, the after-tax cost of borrowing is lower than the cost of capital. Note that there are three projects that are being considered: A, B, and C.

Project A is unambiguously a good deal. Expected returns exceed both the cost of capital and the after-tax borrowing costs. All such projects in this category – and there are not likely to be many – should be undertaken, as they will result in a rising stock price. Investors are being well rewarded for the risks being taken.

Project B is in the middle zone, where expected returns exceed the after-tax cost of borrowing but are less than the cost of capital. Projects in this zone will not be value-enhancing for the firm. That is, they will earn positive accounting returns, but they cannot be justified after considering the risks involved. The stock market will

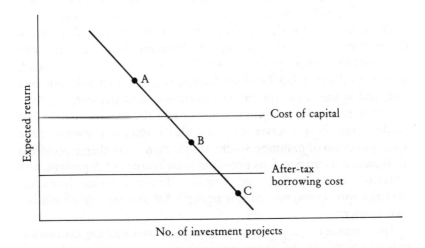

Figure 4.1 Investment project, the cost of capital, and the after-tax cost of borrowing

not pay for such projects.

Projects such as C are a bad deal. They lose money in both accounting terms and in risk-adjusted, economic terms.

The principal that not all money-making projects will add to a firm's value and increase the share price may seem counter-intuitive. One must always remember, though, that everything is relative. The cost of capital is a measure of the returns available from alternative uses of the funds in projects of similar risk. This is the standard that a project must better. It is not enough to show an accounting profit if that profit is less than what could have been earned elsewhere by taking no greater risks.

Beta and the Cost of Capital

The cost of capital is a concept that makes adjustments for risk in evaluating expected returns. Beta is one important measure of risk. Certain methods of calculating the cost of capital make explicit use of beta. While there remains some controversy over various methods of determining a firm's cost of capital, a simple method that highlights the use of beta is presented here.

The cost of capital, essentially being a risk-adjusted, financing cost, requires the use of market interest rates and computed risk premiums in its calculation. Computing the cost of capital involves the determination of three variables: (1) a default-free rate of return, (2) a market risk premium, and (3) a company risk premium.

The first item, the default-free rate of return, can be observed in the marketplace as the yield on US. Treasury debt securities. For corporate investment projects, usually a long-term bond yield, such as that on 20-year US Treasury bonds, is taken as the default-free rate, and in the spring of 1986 this rate was 8.00 percent.

The market risk premium is a measure of the relative riskiness of stocks versus bonds. Over long periods of time, as shown in table 4.1, a portfolio of common stocks would earn more than a portfolio of Treasury securities. This premium is estimated at 5.9 percent, and is known as the market risk premium. There is debate, however, over the appropriateness of this figure – 5.9 percent – in all market environments.

The company risk premium is calculated by adjusting the market risk premium for the company's risk relative to the whole stock market. This is what beta measures. One formula for calculating the company risk premium is as follows:

Company risk premium = (market risk premium) × (beta). (1)

If a company were in the airline industry and had a beta of 1.47, then the computation would work like this:

Company risk premium = (5.9%) × (1.47) = 8.67%. (2)

The final step in the calculation of the cost of capital is simply to add the default-free rate to the company risk premium.

Cost of capital = default-free rate + company risk premium. (3)

or

Cost of capital = 8.00% + 8.67% = 16.67%. (4)

This cost of capital would serve as the hurdle rate for a firm in the airline industry considering expansion within that industry. Projects that were expected to earn returns in excess of this hurdle rate would add value to the company. Projects with expected returns exceeding the firm's after-tax cost of borrowing but not the cost of capital will not increase the firm's stock price, even if accounting earnings rise. The reason is that the project may earn positive returns, but it is too risky.

One final qualification should be noted. Many firms take on projects in different industries. When a diversified firm invests, it must use the cost of capital relevant to the industry in which the new investment will occur, and not the firm's average cost of capital across all lines of business. An example of this was the Coca-Cola Company's acquisition of Columbia Pictures. Coca-Cola is a low-beta firm in a low-beta industry, while Columbia Pictures is a high-beta firm in a high beta industry. In making the acquisition, an appropriate use of this concept would have involved using Columbia Pictures' cost of capital to value the acquisition, and not the much lower cost of capital for the Coca-Cola Company. For Coca-Cola, this has the effect of raising its hurdle rate for expected returns from the acquisition well above the hurdle rate it would normally use for an expansion in its own industry, such as the purchase of a food distributor or beverage bottler.

Summary

Investor objectives and corporate objectives should be linked, and it should come as no surprise that concepts useful for investors are equally useful for corporate executives. The concept of beta and the cost of capital make that linkage explicit.

In the next few chapters a number of corporate finance topics will be examined, from the dividend controversy to mergers and acquisitions. For the most part, these chapters are written from the perspective of the corporation with the objective of maximizing the value of the firm's share price. This perspective contains many lessons for the investor as well, because the job of the investor is no different from that of the corporation, which is to allocate capital among the many choices available.

5

Cooking the Books:
Economics versus Accounting

One of the most difficult tasks faced by equity market investors, as well as senior corporate management, is to derive appropriate measures of a company's financial performance. Investors use performance measures when making judgements about the expected returns and risks the firm is taking as part of the decision process to buy or sell that company's shares. Corporate executives need performance measures to assist them in deciding how to allocate the firm's scarce capital resources, set dividend policy, devise value-enhancing compensation and bonus schemes, evaluate new investment projects, make acquisition decisions, etc.

Investors in US firms have access to a large flow of statistical information, from annual and quarterly reports to the 10–K and 10–Q filings required by the Securities and Exchange Commission (SEC). Senior corporate executives have even greater access to their firm's financial results, presented in a myriad of different ways. The problem is not one of a shortage of data; the issue is how to interpret the information in order to evaluate properly a company's prospects.

A common solution, adopted by both investors and executives, is to use certain financial statistics as all-purpose financial yardsticks. The most common of these is *earnings per share* (EPS). Unfortunately, EPS is purely an accounting measure, and it fails to adjust for a number of critical economic problems bearing on the value of a firm. As a result, EPS as a measure of a firm's performance can be grossly flawed, leading to portfolio errors by investors and management mistakes by corporate executives.

The original version of this article, 'Mis-Accounting For Value', was co-authored with Joel Stern, David Glassman and Bennett Stewart, partners of Stern Stewart and Company, and was published in the company's newsletter, 'Free Cash Flow.'

The interpretation of EPS is a prime example of the clash between accounting concepts and economic concepts. A key theme of this book is the proper understanding of the forward-looking nature of markets as they assess expected risks and returns. Accounting performance measures are by their nature backward-looking, are often distorted by tax regulations, and do not consider risk. A good economic performance measure must look forward, must avoid distortions that do not bear on after-tax wealth, and must consider risk.

In this chapter, a critique of earnings and earnings per share is provided. This critique is set against an economic standard, which explicitly considers risk and return tradeoffs. Specific examples are used to show the misleading nature of EPS as a performance indicator.

Economic Value-added

Economic value, as opposed to accounting measures of value, is determined in the marketplace. The value of publicly held corporations is assessed every trading day by the stock market. Privately held companies, while not having traded shares, are held to the same standards of value when they are bought and sold. The fundamental determinants of value that drive stock prices and corporate value are the same criteria which should be incorporated in any corporate performance measurement process.

Indeed, a wide body of research has demonstrated that the primary determinant of economic value is adequacy of (prospective) corporate returns on total capital employed relative to the cost of obtaining that capital. Corporate returns are based on the cash flows that can be generated by the company's investments. These potential returns are then evaluated against the combined cost of obtaining debt and equity capital (often called the 'hurdle rate'). Economic value is created by investments that provide a return greater than the hurdle rate. Further, the greater the number of these premium investments, the greater will be the total 'economic value-added' and the higher the share price.

Note that the creation of economic value need not be related to winning the competition for business, that is, improving market share. Frequently, division managers commit excessive amounts of capital to achieve only modest improvements in sales. Such a strategy destroys market values. The chief financial officer and chief planning officer also must focus on winning the competition for *capital*. This is achieved by finding investments that earn attractive rates of return after adjusting for risk.

In essence, then, the 'economic' model of the firm emphasizes cash and risk. For example, operating profits must, of course, be reduced for taxes, because taxes involve cash. On the other hand, operating profits would not be reduced for accounting entries that do not involve cash.

Further, consider that financing of the company's assets can be raised in many ways. But each method – debt, equity, or some innovative mixture – requires investors, those providing the capital, to assess the risk of the venture and its probable return. The attractiveness of the prospective return is compared against that available from alternative investments of similar risk. Risk assessment relative to expected return, then, is a key function of the capital allocation and valuation process.

Performance measurement must capture both elements – cash *and* risk. Performance measurement must not be confused by non-cash accounting entries. And measurement procedures must consider risk as well as return when determining economic value.

Earnings and Earnings per Share (EPS)

Such traditional accounting measures as earnings and earnings per share (EPS) can severely distort the true economic picture, misleading investors as to the true prospects for the company. The flaws in these measures emanate both from a failure to measure cash flows properly and a failure to capture the effects of risks. First, they encourage managers to boost earnings with non-cash accounting entries that do not add value. Second, these measures mix finance with business and do not measure risk properly.

Failing to Represent Cash Flow

When the corporate goal is to increase reported earnings or EPS, decisions can be made that harm the economic value of a firm and its investors. And these decisions will result in a lower stock price, in spite of the increase in reported earnings or EPS. There are two classic examples of accounting earnings and EPS failing to represent cash flows, and thus failing to measure value. These are the

LIFO/FIFO decision and the amortization of good will in acquisitions.

LIFO inventory accounting results in lower earnings relative to *FIFO* when inflation is increasing the market value of inventory items. Lower earnings, however, mean lower taxes, and that means a savings of cash. If one compares two companies with exactly the same operating profits before taxes, the LIFO company will report lower earnings than the FIFO company. But the LIFO company will have more cash in the bank at the end of the day, because the lower earnings resulted in lower taxes paid. Which company is worth more? Of course, the one with more cash, not the one with the higher reported earnings. Indeed, an impressive body of stock market research has demonstrated that investors respond favourably to changes from FIFO to LIFO inventory accounting, regardless of the fall in accounting earnings and EPS. (Note: A comprehensive summary of accounting numbers and stock prices appears in "Does It Pay to Manipulate EPS?" by Ross Watts in *The Revolution in Corporate Finance*, Basil Blackwell (1986)).

Equally misleading is the accounting treatment of goodwill in acquisitions. Many companies refuse to undertake acquisitions if pooling of interest accounting cannot be employed. But amortization of goodwill represents neither a cash cost nor a tax shield and, consequently, has no effect on economic value. Again, the evidence indicates that what matters most to investors is the total amount paid relative to the cash flow benefits that are realized. The subsequent accounting recognition of the acquisition is not relevant if it does effect cash or taxes. Managers that are concerned about goodwill write-offs will be biased against strategically sensible acquisitions, and thus may fail to make the appropriate decisions to enhance economic value.

Mixing Finance with Business

Reported earnings and EPS reflect the outcome of financing as well as operating decisions. In the economic model of the firm, value is created by the operating cash flows. Then, financing decisions are made which provide the capital for the operating units and which optimize tax considerations and financial risk. Mixing the operating decisions with the financing can be misleading because of a failure to consider the effects of increased financial risk on the economic value of the firm.

For example, any company can use debt to increase earnings and

EPS as long as the after-tax rate of return on investment exceeds the after-tax cost of borrowing money. With yields on high-grade corporate bonds exceeding 10 percent the after-tax borrowing cost may be as little as 6.6 percent (assuming a 34 percent marginal tax bracket). Corporate investments, including acquisitions, that yield more than 6.6 percent will increase earnings if financed with debt. Unfortunately, this is hardly an acceptable standard of profitability, since it fails to consider risk.

Equity investors do not ignore the additional financial risk they bear when a company increases its leverage. Increased leverage, with its higher required fixed-interest payments, will increase the variability of earnings over a business cycle. The increase in financial risk will lower the price-to-earnings (PE) multiple that investors will assign to the company's stock price.

The original (before increased leverage) PE Multiple will be maintained only if the profits from the new investments cover the full cost of debt and equity financings – because financing with debt today means that equity financing will have to take place in the future (to maintain a prudent capital structure).

Increased leverage can involve tax savings and can be the most appropriate vehicle for financing new investments. The key, however, to adding economic value is not a return that matches the after-tax cost of debt. Instead, returns must be matched against a cost of capital that appropriately accounts for the increased riskiness of the company. Earnings and EPS fall disasterously short in this regard. They assume that the PE multiple will remain constant, and it will not.

Another Look at Risk

Accounting measures are also flawed in their treatment of expenditures for product development and market-building (e.g., R&D, advertising). Accounting rules often require that these outlays be expensed in the year they are incurred, because their future returns are uncertain. Businessmen know, however, that these outlays create value and should be capitalized.

It is true that these expenditures are among the most risky that a company makes, and in many instances the outlays do not pay off. In the aggregate, though, these outlays lay the foundation for the future value of corporations. Investors do not expect every expenditure to pay off, only that there should be enough winners creating enough value to cover the costs of the losers.

To compute the return on their investment, investors relate the cash benefits realized in future years to their initial cash outlays. To be consistent in measuring performance, management should adopt the same 'full-cost' measurement procedure employed by investors. For performance measurement purposes, R&D and market-building expenses should be capitalized, not expensed, as accounting rules prescribe.

Using earnings or EPS as a corporate yardstick encourages management to shy away from the risks associated with new investment. Management's decisions are focused on the near-term costs of value-creating expenditures without proper consideration of the longer-term benefits these expenditures may bring. Thus, the time horizon for payback narrows considerably, putting managers at a disadvantage to more patient competitors. To remedy this, performance measurement must ignore certain accounting conventions and ignore reported EPS. Performance measurement (and management compensation) must be structured to value fairly the long-term benefits of value-creating investments, rather than to focus managers' attention on the near-term costs.

EPS and Acquisitions

Another extremely serious shortcoming of EPS arises when evaluating acquisitions consummated through an exchange of shares. EPS will *always* increase following a merger with a company bearing a lower PE ratio; it will *always* decrease after a merger with a higher-PE-ratio company. Is it therefore logical to conclude that the acquisition of companies with lower PE ratios will always benefit investors, whereas the acquisition of higher PE-ratio-companies will always be harmful? Stated differently, can an acquisition be judged 'good' or 'bad' without knowing whether there are any operating synergies to be realized or if the premium paid is excessive? Instinctively the answer is 'no' but, in fact, the answer is 'yes.'

The reason lies in the fact that PE ratios change in the wake of acquisitions to reflect either an improvement or a deterioration in the overall quality of earnings. The dilution in EPS following the acquisition of a higher multiple company is offset by an increase in the PE multiple, so that the stock price need not be adversely affected. The multiple rises because higher-quality earnings are added to lower-quality earnings. Add high-octane gas to low-octane gas, and the rating will increase. The same is true for earnings.

The opposite happens with the acquisition of a lower multiple company. It is true that EPS will increase, but it is possible that the dilution in the multiple will more than offset it, leading to a lower stock price. Investors care about both the quality and the quantity of earnings in setting stock prices. EPS represents only one half of a two-part equation.

In conclusion, EPS is misleading as a basis for judging the merits of an acquisition with an exchange of shares. Companies that currently sell at high PE ratios can make acquisitions that harm shareholders while at the same time increasing EPS. By diluting their PE ratio, these companies mortgage their future in order to show higher per-share earnings today. Equally questionable is the reluctance of the management of companies selling at modest PE ratios to acquire attractive candidates just because of potential earnings dilution.

Cash, Risk, and EPS

The measurement of corporate performance should always focus on the determinants of economic value, not on purely accounting measures. Economic value is determined by the interplay of cash returns relative to the risks taken. Accounting conventions often involve non-cash (and non-tax) entries. Accounting measures also rarely measure changes in risk. Thus, such favorite accounting standards of measurement as earnings or EPS can be severely flawed and lead to value-damaging rather than value-enhancing decisions.

This article provides just a few examples of the problems that can occur when EPS, rather than economic value, is the standard of judgement. But the principles are straightforward. Never lose sight of cash and risk.

In many ways the Mom-and Pop grocery store understood these concepts all along. What matters is how much cash is in the till at the end of the day relative to the risk taken in the business. A return to the basic of cash and risk can improve substantially the management decision-making process at all firms, no matter what their size, and should also be the focus of investors.

6

The Acquisition Game: How To Tell the Winners from the Losers

Newspaper reports on the most recent merger and acquisition (M&A) activity in the business world tend to be sensationalist. Attention is focused on the sharp rise in the share price of the company being acquired. If the takeover is unfriendly, the story is reported as if it were a major war. This type of journalism often misses or obscures critical issues for investors and corporate management.

M&A activity is simply another example of the financial markets at work reallocating capital from less profitable uses to more profitable ones. To evaluate whether or not this is achieved, attention should be placed on the movement of the share price of the acquiring company – not the company being purchased. The price of the seller's stock is obviously going to rise sharply, because a premium must be paid to gain complete control of a company. But is the price too high? Is the buyer overpaying?

Overpaying

Overpaying for an acquisition is one of the most reliable methods of reducing a company's stock price. One classic example was the $6 fall in the price of DuPont's stock when the acquisition bid for Conoco was announced (see table 6.1). Another was the $2 fall of Xerox stock following the announcement of the bid for Crum and Forster.

A version of this article was prepared jointly with David Glassman, Mark Gressle, Donald Chew, and Bennett Stewart, partners of Stern Stewart and Company, and was originally published in the company's newsletter, 'Free Cash Flow.'

Table 6.1 Negative stock market reaction to acquisitions*

	Price before ($)	Price change ($)	Target's PE
Sohio/Kennecott (3/81)	$54\frac{5}{8}$	$(4\frac{3}{4})$	4
Fluor/St. Joe (3/81)	$49\frac{3}{8}$	(6)	16
Dupont/Conoco (7/81)	$53\frac{3}{8}$	$(6\frac{5}{8})$	7
Xerox/Crum & Forster (9/82)	$32\frac{1}{4}$	$(2\frac{3}{8})$	6

* Most transactions viewed favorably by the market involve companies in closely related businesses with substantial potential synergies.

Table 6.2 Positive stock market reaction to acquisitions

	Price before ($)	Price change ($)	Target's PE
Sears/Dean Witter (10/81)	$16\frac{1}{8}$	$1\frac{1}{4}$	5
General Food/Entenmann's (10/82)	$38\frac{1}{8}$	$6\frac{3}{4}$	N.A.
GTE/Sprint (19/82)	$31\frac{1}{4}$	6	12
Heileman/Pabst (11/82)	$33\frac{1}{2}$	5	loss

Notes: Target's PE had little bearing on stock market reaction. Change in acquirer's stock price, from 1 week prior to 1 week subsequent to announcement.

Had these and other companies understood how the market responds to acquisition pricing, and had these managements known the potential loss of wealth they were inflicting on their shareholders, perhaps the acquisition price would have been lower or the deal shunned.

While the immediate response of the stock market to an acquisition, as measured by the change in the stock price of the acquiring company, may seem to some a rather short-sighted method of judging an acquisition, there is good reason to rely on the market's 'snap' judgement. Sophisticated market players evaluate the total value received by the acquiring company and weigh that value received against the total value paid. And the values paid and received are based on the market's best guess of the long-run performance of the merged companies. The market is taking a view of future performance and placing a value on it today.

While some acquisitions which the market judges as value-damaging do become successful in the long run, others that the market judges as value-enhancing are not successful in the long run. This does not mean that market evaluation of the acquisition should be ignored. Academic research indicates that the market is an 'unbiased predictor' of the success of an acquisition. That is, the market's initial response to an acquisition is a fallible evaluation, but not one that is prone to consistent over- or underestimates of future value. Furthermore, the market's initial evaluation reflects the interplay of many sophisticated investors putting their money on the line. A stock price change provides a measure of the acquisition's value added (or value lost) which managements ignore at their peril and which shareholders, certainly, cannot ignore.

The focus of this article, then, is to examine how to value acquisitions so that one can anticipate whether the acquisition will result in an immediate gain or loss of wealth for the shareholders of the acquiring company. Even in the face of a potentially severe fall in their stock price, some managements will undoubtedly decide to go ahead with value-damaging acquisitions, betting against the market. But prudent managements will make an acquisition bid only after they have carefully considered the likely response that the stock market will inflict on their shareholders if they are perceived to have paid too much.

In a straightforward manner, the stock market's response to an acquisition bid is nothing more than its assessment of whether the total value received by the acquiring company exceeds the total value paid. If the value received fails to measure up to the value surrendered, then the stock price of the acquiring firm falls.

Conceptually, the value received may be divided into two components: (1) the stand-alone value of the target company, and (2) the anticipated value added by the financial and operating benefits of the merger, often known as 'synergy'. The value paid also can be divided into two components: (1) the current market value of the target company, plus (2) the premium paid over the market value. Net value added (lost) is the difference between value received and value paid.

$$Net\ value\ added\ (lost) = value\ received - value\ paid \qquad (1)$$

or,

$$Net\ value\ added\ (lost) = Stand\text{-}alone\ value + synergy \\ - market\ value - premium. \qquad (2)$$

From the arrangement of terms on the right side of equation (2), one can see that value can be created in either of two ways. First, one could identify acquisition targets in which the stand-alone value exceeds the market value. Second, one could seek target firms in which the expected synergies are greater than the premium required.

The first of these methods essentially requires the buyer to discover an 'undervalued' company and acquire it without giving the value away in the premium paid over the market value. A whole host of sophisticated investors is constantly searching for such companies, and rarely does the market so misprice a company that large premiums can be paid and still leave the acquiring firm with any value added. We would be skeptical about bargain hunting as an acquisition strategy. We prefer to begin with the premise that the stand-alone value of the target firm equals its market value, unless a strong case can be made to the contrary. Stated another way, we accept that the market has fairly valued the target company as a stand-alone entity.

Given this assumption, then a value-adding acquisition is one in which the expected synergies exceed the premium paid. And the critical part of evaluating an acquisition is the valuation of the synergies. In general, synergies can be divided into two categories: (1) financial synergies, which include tax and leverage benefits; and (2) operating synergies, which may result from more efficient operations arising from scale increases, improved management, or other business benefits resulting from the merger.

Valuing Financial Synergies

There are two primary sources of financial synergy that deserve explicit treatment: (1) the value of changing the capital structure of the acquiring and the acquired firms, and (2) tax benefits to the acquirer from changes in plant and inventory valuations in the target firm.

Recapitalization Benefits

The structure of an acquisition deal, whether by an exchange of shares, by a cash payment financed by debt, or by some mixture of debt and equity, generally results in a new capital structure for both the acquiring and the acquired firm. This has an immediate impact on the value of both firms separately and on their value as a combined unit.

Capital structure, as embodied in the choice of debt versus equity financing, is an important element in the valuation of a firm, because the interest on debt is tax deductible. The prudent use of debt provides a tax shield that saves cash and adds value. That is, within limits, the use of debt financing effectively reduces the total cost of capital to the firm.

There is, however, a reduction in the firm's financial flexibility that comes with the increase in the debt/equity ratio of the firm. Firms operating in stable businesses can often carry more debt. Firms in high-risk businesses, on the other hand, find that as leverage increases the financial risks that are added are not worth the benefits of a higher tax shield from the use of debt over equity.

Recognizing the role of capital structure in the valuation of a firm leads to several issues in analyzing an acquisition. First, an acquisition may result in a change in the capital structure of the acquiring firm. The acquisition is the motivating force to which the company is responding when it alters its capital structure, but the capital structure could have been changed without the acquisition. The value of the firm would be affected in either case. Second, the acquired firm also may have its capital structure changed after the acquisition. And again, value is affected.

In the first case, where the acquiring firm's capital structure is altered, the value change must be viewed as independent of the acquisition. That is, there are other ways to change a capital structure than by an acquisition financed with debt – share repurchase, for example. Whatever value is created from the capital structure change should not, therefore, be credited to the acquisition.

For example, take a company with 20 percent debt/capital and a current cost of capital of 14.5 percent. Such a company might decide to alter its capital structure to 25 percent debt. Two adjustments must be considered to see the effect on the value of the firm, with everything else remaining unchanged. First, the financial risk of the firm is increased, and this may result in a lower bond rating and a higher interest rate on the firm's new debt. Second, the greater use of debt will save on tax payments. In this case, assuming the company is in a low-risk business, the tax benefits are likely to outweigh the financial risk disadvantages by a wide margin, and typically might reduce the cost of capital to 14 percent from the original 14.5 percent. For a firm valued on the stock market at $1 billion, a reduction of 50 basis points in the cost of capital could result in an increase in total value of over $30 million.

When a relatively unleveraged company makes a large acquisition financed by adding debt, the change in the capital structure of the firm can easily be more dramatic than the previous example. And if the immediate change in the capital structure is viewed as a permanent change, then the stock market will reflect the full value of the increased use of debt. This value should not be attributed to the acquisition, since the capital structure could have been altered without making the acquisition. To do so would incorrectly mix the financing decision (capital structure) with the investment decision (whether to make the acquisition).

The second recapitalizing effect is felt on the value of the target firm. If this recapitalization creates value, then this value can be appropriately used to justify the payment of a given premium over market value for the target firm.

When the target is acquired, it will come under the umbrella of the acquiring firm. Essentially, the target firm is recapitalized with the new debt structure of the parent firm. If a company uses debt to acquire a target, and the use of debt, including the consolidated position of the target, takes the company to a 25 percent debt/total capital ratio, then the target company must be revalued using the 25 percent ratio. This holds regardless of what the capital structure of the target company was before it was acquired.

If the target company's stand-alone use of debt stood at, say, 10 percent, less than that of the acquiring company's new capital structure, then the new value of the target company is likely to exceed its old value. Suppose the target company moves from a 10 to 25 percent debt structure. If the original cost of capital for the target was 15.0 percent, the increase in the debt ratio will lower the cost of capital to 14.0 percent. If the target was worth about $250 million in a stand-alone value, then the recapitalization benefit would be around $20 million. This is an example of financial synergy that is properly included in the acquisition.

As an aside, what may be happening when the target company is recapitalized at a higher debt ratio is that the acquirer is using the debt capacity of the target firm to finance the acquisition. Hence a corollary point is that, to avoid a takeover, a potential target firm should maintain a high debt load.

Tax Synergies

In most acquisitions tax synergies are very important, and in leveraged buyouts they are critical. Benefits to the acquirer arise because the target firm's inventories and plant and equipment can be revalued to save cash through tax reductions.

By writing up the value of inventories of the target firm, the acquiring firm reduces the taxable income that results when the inventories are sold. In some industries this can be a very substantial benefit. Also, the plant and equipment of the target company can be revalued at fair market value rather than at the historical costs as carried on the books of the target firm. This write-up of plant and equipment values then leads directly to higher depreciation charges, saving cash taxes. Depending on the form of acquisition, these write-ups may also trigger a recapture tax liability, but generally the benefits outweigh the costs.

These tax benefits are not available to the target firm as a stand-alone entity. But at the time of the acquisition, the acquiring firm can allocate a portion of the premium it is paying to writing-up the asset values. For example, in the case of the Brown–Forman acquisition of Lenox, the tax synergies represented around $29 million. As can be seen, tax synergies can be very substantial.

Operating Synergies

Compared to the financial synergies, which can be calculated in a straightforward way, the operating synergies involve extensive judgement. The judgement comes in selecting the forward plan of the target company on which to place a value.

The market has placed a value on the target firm as a stand-alone entity. But the acquiring firm often feels that, through economies of scale, improved management, increased marketing strength, or any of a variety of operating factors, the target firm will produce a higher cash flow in the years after the acquisition than was possible as a stand-alone entity. The value of these increased cash flows represents the value ascribed to operating synergies.

In many cases, it pays to work backward from the price of the acquisition to determine the implicit value being placed on operating synergies. For example, an acquiring firm may offer a 50 percent premium over today's share price to acquire the target firm. Based on relatively well defined financial synergies, as described in previous sections, an offer of a 30 percent premium can be justified. The remaining premium must be justified by operating synergies. And if it is not, then the stock price of the acquiring firm will decline when the acquisition is announced.

In other words, one can calculate how well the target firm must do in coming years for the premium to just equal the value received. That is, the forward plan that must be achieved for the acquisition simply to break even in value terms can be examined to see if it is possible to achieve. And of course, if the operating synergies just equal the required amount, then the stockholders of the acquiring company are neither hurt nor helped. The stockholders of the target company get all the gains.

Operating synergies, because they involve the most judgement, are the prime areas to scrutinize before making an acquisition. In almost every case, there are substantial financial synergies for the acquiring company. But a healthy premium is paid to the target company's stockholders. Operating synergies must exceed the difference between the two previous factors, which are relatively 'hard' numbers, before value can be created for the stockholders of the acquiring firm.

Calculating what is required in future performance by the target firm to justify a given premium can help immensely in avoiding value-damaging acquisitions. If the numbers look reasonable, then the acquisition may make good sense. But in many cases, the implied forward plan appears much too optimistic for the stock market to bear, and the immediate result is that the market writes down the value of the acquiring firm.

Don't Give Away the Store

By comparing the total value received to the total value paid, the acquiring firm can make an educated guess as to the effect of an acquisition on its share price. Even where the financial synergies look compelling and operating synergies seem obvious, the deal will harm the shareholders of the acquiring company if the premium paid exceeds the value of the financial and operating synergies. What has happened is that all the benefits of the acquisition (plus some) have been captured by the shareholders of the target firm: there is nothing left over, in terms of value added, for the shareholders of the acquiring firm. This framework is illustrated in Figures 6.1 and 6.2.

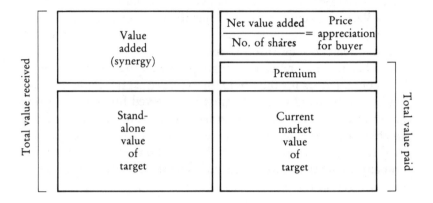

Figure 6.1   Net value added increases the stock price of the buyer.

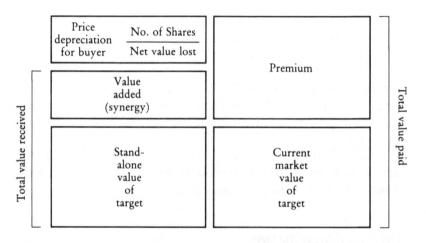

Figure 6.2   Net value lost decreases the stock price of the buyer.

It does not have to be this way. For example, when GTE acquired Sprint, GTE's stock price rose, as did the stock price of Southern Pacific, the seller from whom GTE bought Sprint. The acquisition made good business sense, and the deal was arranged so that both the buyer and the seller shared the benefits.

In the case of Heileman Breweries acquiring Pabst, again, the share price of the both the buyer and the seller rose after the announcement of the merger. The operating synergies made business sense, and the value added was split between the buyer and seller.

Acquisitions are not generally zero sum games. Value is created, but the question is, Who gets it? If the acquiring company gets caught in a bidding war and allows emotions to rule, then the target company's shareholders may get all the benefits and then some. The shareholders of the acquiring company must shoulder this burden.

On the other hand, if the acquiring company makes an objective evaluation of the financial synergies and avoids an acquisition price that implies a terribly unrealistic forward plan for the target company, then the acquirer will know when to drop out of the bidding and let the deal collapse. To add value for the stockholders, management cannot allow itself to give away the store.

7

Talk to Me:
Financial Communication

What information should investors demand from corporations? What information should corporations be willing to provide? Interestingly enough, the answers to these questions should be the same, as long as the maximization of the value of the firm is the common goal of both the shareholders and management.

Shareholders need certain information to appreciate fully management's forward plan and to give that plan full value in today's market. Financial markets are forward-looking. Investors focus on expected returns, which are weighed against perceived risks. By carefully explaining the plans and policies that will guide a company's growth, and thereby building credibility with investors through quality financial communication, tomorrrow's share price can be achieved before the performance is delivered.

Achieving tomorrow's share price today should be a goal of management's financial communications program. Not only are shareholders rewarded, but the corporation's business plan may be enhanced as well. Where stock or options are used in bonus plans, management is compensated directly for creating value. An attractive stock price allows the corporation to finance new investments through the issuance of new shares without penalizing old shareholders by cutting in new ones at a 'low' price. And, last, but certainly not least, a high share value is the best defense against an unwanted takeover offer.

Thus, companies should not view financial communication as a battle to disclose as little information as possible to shareholders.

A version of this article was co-authored with Joel Stern, David Glassman and Bennett Stewart, partners of Stern Stewart and Company, and was originally published in the company's newsletter, 'Free Cash Flow,' as 'Achieving Tomorrow's Stock Price Today.'

The essence of financial communication should be to provide the financial markets with the information needed to assess the company's future performance. It is in the company's interest to provide this information, and it is in investor's interests to obtain it. This chapter discusses a variety of issues in corporate financial communications. Guidelines for financial information are developed to meet twin goals. They provide a systematic way in which corporations should handle financial disclosure. And they provide a set of criteria through which investors can evaluate a company's future prospects. As long as the mutual goal of shareholders and management is to maximize the value of the firm, the guidelines will apply to both groups.

A key concept is that the right way for corporations to approach financial communication, and the approach that is likely to yield the highest share price, involves an understanding of how the market sets share prices. Many of the themes emphasized in the introductory chapters of this book – risk-return tradeoffs and market efficiency and expectations – play a critical role. Using this framework of understanding how financial markets work, one can set guidelines for financial communication and identify common misconceptions.

Speak to the Lead Steers

Share values are not set through a polling technique where all investors have an equal say in what the price should be. Stock prices, like all prices, are set at the margin, not by the average investor, but by the smartest money in the game. The herd is influenced by a set of large, influential investors – 'Lead Steers,' we call them – who take a sophisticated view of firms and who care about long-run performance in terms of cash flow and risk.

Take the grain markets as an example. The largest companies, such as Cargill and Bunge, are on top of the market all of the time, studying it and analyzing it. And they go to the market and buy and sell grain based on their extensive research and knowledge of the market. If you or I were also to buy grain, on say the Chicago Board of Trade, would we pay any different price than Cargill or Bunge? The lead steer investors have established the price using all the available information, and that is the price at which anyone can buy grain.

A few facts about the stock market may help to demonstrate that the importance of the supposedly naive retail investor is vastly overrated. In 1982, the number of trades on the Big Board represented by 100-share orders – the typical sign of the little investor – fell below 2 percent for the first time. Another startling fact is that exchange members trading for themselves now account for more volume than the entire retail public. Furthermore, institutional trading in blocks of 10,000 shares or more now makes up more than 40 percent of the market. And, contrary to popular opinion, facts demonstrate that the absence of the retail customer on the American Stock Exchange and the Over-The-Counter market is even more pronounced than on the Big Board.

Widows and orphans do not set stock prices. It is lead steer against lead steer, making calculated decisions based on all available information, that determines prices in today's highly sophisticated financial markets.

How Do Lead Steers Get Information?

First and foremost, lead steer investors do not rely on a company's reported accounting results. If accounting statements were all that mattered, stock prices would change just four times a year – when quarterly results were released. Stock prices move daily, though, as lead steers compete to ferret out new, and potentially profitable, information.

Lead steer investors talk to customers, suppliers, and competitors to discover important developments early. To get an idea of the lengths to which lead steers will go to procure information, an article taken from the pages of the *Wall Street Journal* illustrates the point. The article is entitled, 'IBM Watchers Process Data on the Big Firm To Divine Its Program,' and it chronicles how information on the computer giant is obtained in ways that even IBM cannot prevent.

The article indicates that one analyst 'was able to predict IBM's re-entry into the computer services business after a ten year absence. "We got information they were transferring high-level software and marketing people to a secret project in Orlando," he says. "A couple of guys didn't want to move, and they talked. And then IBM did a lot of hiring down there." '

In a more recent example, analysts were able to estimate that IBM would ship up to 2 million personal computers in 1984, based on the company's orders for components. The anecdotes and the academic research both support the same conclusion: lead steers are uncannilly smart in learning about corporate performance through channels other than published financial reports.

Lead Steers See Through Accounting Results

When lead steer investors scrutinize accounting reports, they look through the numbers to see the cash-generating potential of the business and the risk in the business. Accounting tricks do not fool this group.

Take the LIFO versus FIFO debate. In inventory accounting when prices are rising (as in the 1970s), companies using LIFO (last in, first out) will report lower earnings then FIFO (first in, first out) companies. If reported earnings matter, than FIFO companies should outperform LIFO companies. But the LIFO company, by reporting less earnings, also pays less taxes. This saves cash. Would lead steers miss that important fact? No!

The *Wall Street Journal* reported on the research of University of Chicago's Professor Sunder, who compared firms that switched to LIFO with FIFO firms. 'The FIFO firms obviously reported higher earnings than they otherwise would have, but their stocks did not outperform the market over a two-year span centered on the public announcement of the change.'

Extensive research has also been conducted on other accounting issues, including purchase versus pooled accounting for acquisitions, the introduction of FASB #8 for foreign exchange translation, switching from deferred to flow-through methods of accounting for investment tax credits, and changing from straight-line to accelerated methods for book depreciation. In every instance, the conclusion has been the same. The market is not fooled by accounting changes that inflate earnings without improving cash flow, and when cash is affected, stock prices follow the cash, not the accounting earnings.

Selling Soap and Selling Stock

Many senior officials of major corporations believe that their common stock can be marketed like any other product. Their business experience has taught them that profits depend on carefully selecting a target market, differentiating the product, and increasing demand through advertising. They see no reason why these same principles should not be applied to promote the company's stock.

To do so, public relations firms are hired, often at great expense, to tell the company's story through slick advertisements. The annual report is carefully crafted to sell the company and its management. In short, the company is hyped in the best Madison Avenue tradition.

There are serious pitfalls here. Whether or not it is recognized as such, an important assumption behind these practices is that there are a fixed number of common shares outstanding, so that any increase in demand will require a higher stock price to allocate the available supply among potential investors. It does not work this way in the stock market, and stock cannot be sold like soap.

An extensive publicity campaign may persuade more investors to purchase the company's stock, but this need not mean a higher stock price. If lead steer investors remain convinced that the company's intrinsic value is unchanged, then they will sell their stock on any price rises – preventing any price rise. The stock will be more actively traded, but its price will not change.

Investors have many choices in arranging their portfolios. Stock can be bought or sold short. Stocks of related companies, with similar expected returns and risk, can be bought or sold. Portfolios can be constructed with Treasury bills and stock index funds to achieve certain risk–return criteria. In sum, the ability of the lead steers to substitute within their portfolio means that *their* view of instrinsic value, not Madison Avenue hype, will determine the share price. Hype can alter volume and can change the investor mix, but it cannot change the share price unless *new* information about company prospects is being provided to the market. The rule that applies is as follows: if the company's problem is on Wall Street, Madison Avenue cannot help.

Dividends as Financial Communication

One of the most expensive forms of financial communication used by firms is dividend policy. When companies wish to communicate how well they are doing, they raise their dividend. When times are bad, they confirm the worst by cutting the dividend. In essence, these companies have trained the market, and the lead steers, to watch the dividend policy for information about how management views the future prospects of the firm.

This training process is not unusual. Financial analyists are used to looking for clues anywhere they can find them, and by their behaviour, companies can condition the market. Fed-watchers have this problem, because the Federal Reserve is so secretive. *Business Week* magazine once asked a group of Fed-watchers why, with all the problems in the money supply data, they persisted in watching it so closely. They replied that the Fed attached importance to the money supply, so they watched it. Furthermore, they said, if the Fed watched egg salad production, so would they.

If companies attach importance to dividend policy announcements, then so will the market. But the reason is not that dividends matter: the reason is that they are a form of financial communication. There is extensive research to indicate that investors prefer capital gains as opposed to dividends, because dividends are taxed at a higher rate than capital gains and investors can borrow against the appreciated value of their shares while deducting the interest from their taxes. At best, one can argue that many lead steer investors, namely pension funds and the like, do not pay taxes, and hence are neutral. In all cases, however, what the lead steer investor seeks is after-tax, total return on dividends plus capital appreciation.

The case that higher dividends help a stock's price cannot be made on a corporate finance basis. It can be made only on financial communication grounds. And saddling a company with a high dividend payout, essentially a fixed cost, just to tell the world it is doing well is an expensive and inefficient form of financial communication.

The same case can be made for managements that view consistently rising earnings as the way to a higher stock price. By using available accounting conventions, they report quarter after quarter of earnings increases. But this can be an expensive form of financial communication, too. It can prevent the company from taking short-run earnings declines that are part of long-run, attractive investment strategies.

For example, take the case of Verbatim Corporation, a maker of floppy disks for computers. The president once told a group of security analysts that his company would experience a period of declining earnings for the first time, not because of poor performance, but because of the costs incurred in opening a major new plant. He stated that he was not concerned with the earnings decline, and that if the analysts were they could recommend other stocks. He claimed that his management team was convinced that the overall return on investment would be attractive, and for this reason the investment made sense no matter what the near-term accounting impact was. Following this statement, Verbatim's stock price climbed rapidly. Unbroken records of earnings growth are important only when management trains the market to read financial communications into them.

Effective Financial Communication

What, then, constitutes a quality and cost-effective financial communications program? Unlike financial disclosure of account-ing results, which concentrates on the past and often confuses reported results with actual cash results, financial communications must concentrate on the future. The goal, after all, is to have tomorrow's performance incorporated into today's stock price. And, contrary to financial hype, which targets the retail market, effective financial communication aims at the sophisticated inves-tors – the lead steers – who can deliver tomorrow's stock price today.

More specifically, companies must provide information about the factors that actually create value. Researchers have identified six factors that have a critical bearing on how the the market prices stocks. While there are more factors that may be involved, these six capture the essence of the stock pricing process. And, of the six factors, four are under the direct influence of management. An effective financial communications program will make these four factors its centerpiece.

They are as follows:

1. the net operating profits, after taxes and before financing costs (NOPAT), that the business can be expected to earn over the business cycle. Notice that operating results explicitly are separated from financing considerations;
2. new investment spending that is anticipated, where investment includes additions to working capital as well as capital expendi-tures;
3. the anticipated rate of return, in relevant cash flow terms over the lives of the new investments. Items 2 and 3, then, summarize the new opportunities the company has;
4. the company's target capital structure. With interest payments tax deductible, debt is cheaper than equity, and the prudent use of debt can add value to the firm. Investors need to be informed

of the level of debt that the company considers ideal, so that temporary deviations will not be misinterpreted.

The other two factors that are important to investors, but are less controllable by management are:

5. the degree of risk in the company's major lines of business and the current level of interest rates. These factors establish the minimum return required by investors for each business activity, commonly known as the cost of capital;
6. the length of time that investors expect management to take to find and make attractive new investments. After some time, competitive market forces tend to erode even proprietary returns and make management's job of locating attractive new opportunities in the same business areas more difficult.

While these six factors can serve as a framework for financial communications, other related factors should also be considered. These include the following:

1. acquisition–divestiture strategy. At a minimum, investors need to know what guidelines management is using in seeking acquisitions, and equally important are the criteria for disposing of businesses;
2. management's incentive compensation plan. Investors understand that, where management is paid according to value creation, shareholders' interest will be paramount. When bonuses focus on earnings per share or other accounting measures, shareholder interest and management interests may diverge;
3. business risk management policies. Investors need to understand the exposure of the company to various business risks. Accordingly, management should disclose the basic framework of its contracts with its employees, customers, suppliers, and partners;
4. international performance. Nowhere are accounting numbers more misleading than in presenting international results. Management should explain how it evaluates its overseas operations and how it manages the related currency exposure;
5. financing policies. In addition to communicating the target debt/equity ratio, management should indicate the criteria it uses in choosing among various instruments from preferred stock to convertibles. Furthermore, management should explain how the company's dividend policy relates to its financial policy. Finally, investors should be apprised of the company's pension fund

policy, including the assumptions used in determining the pension fund liability.

Obviously, to be really effective, financial communication must go to the heart of the company's planning process. The only way to build credibility in the market and to achieve tomorrow's stock price today is to convince the market that the company has a well-conceived plan for the future. Furthermore, investors know that management decisions to communicate or not to communicate these planning issues often say a lot about the planning process itself, how well the company is managed, and how much the company's management is really in control of the company's destiny. This is why effective financial communication is critical to instill investors' confidence in management.

Effective financial communication should be part of the overall planning process. It can eliminate the need to use more costly and inflexible forms of communication, such as dividend policy. It makes the company's actions more predictable to the market, and the market always extracts a discount for uncertainty.

There are no tricks; lead steers are too smart. But by communicating the information that lead steers need to know to properly value the company, the company has a much better chance of having its forward plan fairly valued by the market. In other words, the company can achieve tomorrow's stock price today, to the benefit of both managers and investors.

8
An On-going Controversy: Why Pay Dividends?
Donald Chew

If you take a close look at the growth stocks that have consistently outperformed the Dow Jones Industrial Average over the years, many of these stocks pay little or no dividends. A number of these stocks are over-the-counter (OTC), high-growth, high-technology stocks, and we all know that such companies can get away without paying high, or indeed any, dividends. But consider the cases of more staid companies like Capital Cities Communications and the Gleason Company. Capital Cities pays a dividend of 20 cents, offering an effective annual yield of less than 0.2 percent. It is in a very old business: publications and other communications. The Gleason Company (formerly Gleason Works) manufactures auto parts and pays no dividend. Do such companies, and their investors, suffer from management's decision to retain earnings rather than paying them out? The answer coming from professional researchers at premiere business schools appears to be a forthright 'No.'

Over the past 15 or 20 years, the question of the effect of dividends on stock prices has become a controversial one. Among finance scholars today, there are only two positions on the dividend question that are seriously defended: (1) that dividends are 'irrelevant' (that is, whether companies retain their earnings or pay them out to stockholders is a matter of indifference to investors in aggregrate); and (2) that dividends are actually harmful to taxable investors, because prior to the Tax Reform Act of 1986 individual investors had to pay higher taxes on dividends than on capital gains.

Donald Chew is a partner in the firm of Stern Stewart & Company (New York), and this article was originally published in the company's newsletter, 'Free Cash Flow.' The authors of this volume appreciate Don Chew's granting permission for this article to be reprinted here.

Dividends Are Irrelevant

The smart investor – and there are plenty of them around – is concerned not just about the dividend yield, but about his total return: dividends plus capital gains. Although some investors need current income to pay their bills, the investors that dominate the market – those that move the market and set stock prices – are really concerned only about total return. (They are also, of course, concerned about how those returns will be taxed.)

As long as there are efficient capital markets, those stockholders requiring income can get their hands on cash simply by selling shares. Investors, on the whole, should not be willing to pay higher prices for high-dividend shares just because they provide a slightly more convenient means of getting cash.

This means, setting tax consequences aside for a moment, that a dollar paid out in dividends is simply a dollar lost in capital gains. This principle can be seen at work when companies trade on the ex-dividend date: when the shares go ex-dividend, their stock price typically falls by an amount roughly equal to the dividend-per-share paid out to investors.

From corporate management's point of view, the dividend payout is really just another means of liquidating the company's assets. If the company pays out a very high proportion of its earnings, it will be able to finance future growth only by raising more money through a new debt or stock offering. For this reason, unless a company is repeatedly announcing new debt or stock issues (like AT&T, for example, when it is about to go through a new growth phase), you can interpret a high dividend yield as the sign of a mature, if not, indeed, stagnant company.

Public utilities, for example, have the highest dividend yields going, and there are good reasons for it. Their rates are set by state commissions, which are designed to allow them to earn a 'fair' rate of return on invested capital. But no more. Companies grow rapidly only when they face prospects of highly profitable returns. Utility companies, because they are so regulated, do not offer the promise of abnormally high rates of return on capital. Therefore, their incentive is not to retain their earnings and invest in expansion, but instead to distribute their earnings to stockholders.

Utilities are thus a low-risk, low-return investment. You will never get rich investing in utilities. If consumer causes restrict utilities' ability to raise their rates, you may indeed lose, although probably not a lot.

It is a mistake, at any rate, to think that utilities are less risky *because* they pay high dividends. If you think this way, you are failing to consider that it's the total return – dividends plus capital appreciation – that should matter. Utilities, as you've probably noticed, resort more to new stock and debt offerings than do companies in any other industry. This is not because they are contemplating new investment. It's because they have paid all that cash out to investors, and now they have to retrieve it. They are simply recycling cash. And as anyone who has held utility stocks over the past ten years will confirm, the process of recycling does not add greatly to stockholder wealth.

This does not mean, however, that utilities *should not* pay high dividends. It simply reflects management's judgement about the prospects for utilities in a highly regulated environment. Rather than invest large amounts of cash in projects, like nuclear power, where the risks appear to greatly outweigh the rewards, utility executives seem to have collectively determined that it is better to distribute earnings to investors, who can then *choose* to reinvest, or place the cash in more promising investments – with a better risk-reward tradeoff.

In this sense, then, a company's *refusal* to pay a dividend may actually signal management's optimism about the future. They are saying: 'We have good prospects, and we need the funds for growth. You, the investor, are better served by allowing us to keep your money than by returning it to you to stash in a money market fund.'

We also know, of course, that announcements of dividends cut or passed are not well received by the market. But this is not because of dividends *per se*. The negative response to dividend reductions is really in response to the negative *information* released by such announcements. Reduced dividends means diminished earnings prospects for the future.

Dividends and Risk

What this boils down to, then, is that, although *changes* in the dividend matter to the market, the *level* of the dividend does not affect stock prices. It can be used to provide a fairly reliable, though not infallible, guide to the relative risk of investments in companies. This is because risky companies – those whose earnings, and stock prices, fluctuate from year to year – tend to pay out a significantly lower percentage of earnings than their less risky counterparts.

Risky companies do this for a good reason: to the extent that management refuses to cut the dividend, dividends really represent a fixed cost of the business. Risky businesses are already risky, because they have a large proportion of fixed to variable costs. So when the economy, the demand for their products (and thus their revenues), turns down, their costs remain high, squeezing profits. Such companies wisely restrict the dividend.

But it is important to recognize that higher dividends do not *cause* lower risk: they simply *reflect* the level of corporate risk. They are not the reason why the proverbial 'widows and orphans' typically hold shares of public utilities. The risks of utilities, and indeed of all companies, are determined by how vulnerable their earnings power is to changes in the economy: Risk is not affected by management's decision to pay out or reinvest earnings.

It is true, of course, that dividends are more predictable than capital gains. They are subject to the control of management, not to the vagaries of the market.

This is the popular 'bird in the hand' argument. It says, in effect, 'Well, even if the market goes down, at least I'll have a stable return from dividends over the lean years.' The flaw in this argument is the failure to recognize that a dollar paid in per-share dividends means that the stock price will have fallen a dollar lower than otherwise. Dividends are paid out of earnings, and it's earnings, or the expectation of future earnings, that drive stock prices.

Dividends Can Hurt

The only serious challenge to the dividend 'irrelevance' proposition comes from those who believe dividends hurt. The main argument of the 'anti-dividend' school of thought is, as suggested initially, a tax argument.

To understand the tax argument, the taxation of dividends and capital gains before and after the passage of the Tax Reform Act of 1986 must be made clear. Dividends received by investors are taxed as ordinary income. Until recently, the highest marginal rate was 70 percent in the United States. This was reduced in the tax cut of 1982 to 50 percent and then reduced again to 28 percent (33 percent for certain income brackets) in the Tax Reform Act of 1986. Prior to the Tax Reform Act of 1986, long-term capital gains were given a 60 percent exclusion before being taxed at regular rates. This made the maximum capital gains tax equal to 20 percent when marginal tax rates were 50 percent. Under the Tax Reform Act of 1986, capital gains are taxed as ordinary income, just like dividends, with no exclusions.

Prior to the Tax Reform Act of 1986, therefore, the tax on dividends was substantially higher than the tax on long-term capital gains for most investors. In many countries there is no tax on capital gains. This obviously matters to investors, giving them a significant preference for capital gains over dividends. To illustrate the argument with a very simple example, assume that there are only two companies available to investors, and that they have identical earnings prospects. Company A is expected to pay out all its earnings in dividends forever. Company B will never pay a dividend, but will distribute its earnings to stockholders in the form of non-taxable stock repurchases. Assume also that all investors are taxed at 50 percent on dividends, and (as in many countries) pay no taxes on capital gains. In such a world, company A could be worth exactly one-half of company B. Or, to view it a little differently, company A would have to earn twice as much as company B to sell at the same price.

Going back to the real world, this example means that investors, in order to earn the same return after tax, must expect to earn a higher total return (dividends plus appreciation) on high-dividend stocks than on equivalently risky, low-dividend stocks. And, in order to offer a higher total return, high-dividend stocks must sell at *lower prices* than otherwise.

Finance scholars have attempted to test this argument by measuring the total returns of high- versus low-paying stocks over time. And though there are some remaining problems of method, all the tests provide at least some support for the anti-dividend argument.

With the passage of the Tax Reform Act of 1986, dividends and capital gains are treated alike in the United States and both are taxed at an individual's marginal tax rate. This effectively removes the tax-based argument against the payment of dividends in the United States, although not in many other countries. Also, with the increasing domination of the market by large tax-exempt institutions like pension funds and insurance companies, tax considerations are probably not as important. And investors can avoid taxes on dividends by offsetting this income with interest on borrowings, or other tax shelters.

Total After-tax Return Is What Counts

The long and short of dividends, then, is that they don't really matter. They are merely one way of slicing the pie of a company's market value. It is true they can be used as a guide to management's intentions, and to the risk of your investment. But this is because managements have based the dividend not only on past earnings, but also on the future earnings and investment prospects of the company.

The total return, nonetheless, is what counts. The value of the corporation is determined by profits, expectations of future earnings. Dividends are merely a means of distributing the proceeds. And if investors are not successful in neutralizing tax effects, dividends may actually be shrinking the size of the corporate pie – by cutting the government in.

Part III
Bond Markets

9

A Question of Leadership: Why the Bond Market Drives the Stock Market

Events that affect the bond market directly, such as declines in inflationary expectations leading to lower interest rates, can have an equally powerful effect on the equity markets. Essentially, bonds and stocks are competing investments. At any given time, investors can choose between a portfolio of bonds and one of equities, or some mix of the two. As competing investments, when the prospects for returns change in one market, the other market can be affected as well.

This chapter is devoted to making explicit the link between bond and stock markets. The purpose is to show how changes in interest rates drive the stock market. The key to this deduction lies in understanding how different investments compete against one another for investors' capital.

The Opportunity Cost of Investing in Stocks

Suppose a stock is expected to return 15 percent annually (capital appreciation plus dividends). Suppose, further, that another investment of similar risk is at first expected to return 15 percent; but, as economic events change, its expected annual return increases to 20 percent. In such a case, when the expected return on the alternative investment increases, its price will move up relative to the first investment.

Another way to view this relationship is to think of the bond

Many of the ideas in this article were originally contained in a research paper jointly prepared with Joel Stern and released to the clients of Stern, Stewart and Company in 1982.

market as the opportunity cost of investing in the stock market. That is, if you had $1 million to invest, putting all of it into the equity markets would mean that opportunities to earn returns in the bond market would be foregone. This is what is meant by an opportunity cost – the cost of lost opportunities. As the opportunity cost rises, more investors will be reluctant to pay the cost, that is, to forego the opportunity to invest in bonds. In this sense, changes in bond prices, which reflect changes in interest rates, can be thought of as changes in the opportunity cost of investing in stocks. And changes in this cost will change the investment strategies of at least some investors.

Stocks versus Bonds

The opportunity cost relationship can be used to explain, in broad terms, the movement of the stock market relative to interest rates and the bond market. The level of the Dow Jones Industrial Average (DJIA), the best-known index of general US stock prices, is influenced most directly by two factors:

1. expected corporate profitability, and
2. the opportunity cost of investors' funds (as reflected in rates of returns on competing investments, such as bonds).

The latter factor, adjusted for the differences in the riskiness of two competing investments, can be thought of as the minimum return that corporations must earn if stock prices are to rise. In other words, if expected corporate profitability does not exceed returns available on alternative investments, such as bonds (adjusted for risk), stock prices will not rise. Investors will prefer bonds to stocks.

Expressed in a simple formula, the relationship between these two factors and stock prices is as follows:

$$DJIA = \frac{Corporate\ profitability\ index}{Required\ return\ based\ on\ alternative\ investment} . (1)$$

In this formula, corporate profitability can be measured by companies' return on invested capital. (The return on stockholders' equity reported in most annual reports is a good measure of corporate profitability.)

Required returns, or the returns on alternative investments, are most easily approximated by interest rates. For simplicity, the yield on long-term US government bonds is a useful measure. To compare two investments, however, the risk characteristics must be similar. Since the riskiness of common stocks is widely accepted as exceeding the riskiness of US Treasury securities, a risk premium must be added to the expected return on the US government bonds before comparing returns. Extensive academic research, based on decades of statistical observations, has indicated that an estimated risk premium of about 6 percent should be added to the Treasury bond yield to achieve an appropriate comparison to common stocks. (Please note: one can take a different view of the appropriate risk premium and still apply the model developed here to show the relationship between interest rates and the stock market.)

When interest rates fall, so do required returns. If we hold investor expectations of corporate profitability constant, then clearly this will result in a rise in the stock prices. When interest rates rise, required returns rise and, holding expectations of corporate profitability constant, stock prices fall.

Case Studies: 1982–3 and 1985–6

The great stock market rallies of 1982–3 and 1985–6 are prime examples of declining interest rates driving the equity markets to new highs. To see the power of interest rates on stock prices, some simple numerical examples are very useful.

First, we must start our example by constructing the base index for corporate profitability. The corporate returns index is a calculated index starting from an arbitrary base period. For our examples, we will start with the period in the fall of 1980 when the Dow Jones Industrial Average was trying to break 1000 and US Treasury bonds were yielding 11 percent. With these numbers, we can calculate a starting point for our profitability index as follows. Starting with the basic formula, equation (1), we turn it around: from

$$DJIA = (Required\ returns)\ /\ (Profitability\ index) \qquad (1)$$

to

$$Profitability\ index = (DJIA) \times (Required\ returns) \qquad (2)$$

Then we insert our initial conditions of a 1000 DJIA, and 11 percent government bond yield, and a 6 percent risk adjustment:

$$\textit{Corporate profitability index} = (1000) \times (0.11 + 0.06) \quad (3)$$

or

$$\text{Corporate profitability index} = 170 \quad (4)$$

Now, suppose the long-term US Treasury bond yields rise to 15 percent, as they did in the spring of 1982. Then, holding the corporate profitability constant, the direct effect on the DJIA is easily seen:

$$DJIA = (170)/(0.15 + 0.06) = (170)/(0.21) = 810. \quad (5)$$

The move of 4 percentage points, from 11 to 15 percent, in the bond yield accounted for a 190-point drop in the Dow Jones Industrial Average. And this did not include any drop in corporate profitability.

But such an interest rate increase was probably associated with expectations of a recession and a drop in corporate profits, both of which actually occurred in 1981 and 1982. If corporate profits dropped 10 percent, the corporate profitability index would have fallen from 170 to 153 (i.e., $170 \times (1.00 - 0.10) = 170 \times 0.90 = 153$). With bond yields still at 15 percent, this implies a DJIA of 729, calculated as follows:

$$DJIA = (153)/(0.15 + 0.65) = (153)/(0.21) = 729. \quad (6)$$

The DJIA never fell to this low level, but it did touch the 780s before interest rates started to decline.

Remember, these numbers are just an illustration of the interest rate effect on stock prices, not a precise prediction.

To get an idea of the magnitude of the effect of falling interest rates on stock prices, suppose bond yields drop from 15 to 10 percent – a 5-point decline, which occurred in the second half of 1982:

$$DJIA = (153)/(0.10 + 0.06) = (153)/(0.16) = 956. \quad (7)$$

The only difference between the calculations in equations (6) and (7) was the drop in bond yields, since corporate profits were held constant. This indicates that the 5-percentage-point drop in bond yields translated into a greater than 200-point move in the DJIA, without a change in expected corporate profitability. This corresponds to the major market move in the latter half of 1982, from below 800 to close to 1000, which occurred before the economy began to grow and profits began to rise.

Declining interest rates, particularly rates of this magnitude, can exert a powerful stimulatory effect on the economy and corporate profits. As the US economy began to rebound strongly from the recession in 1983, corporate profitability expectations rose sharply as well. A 30 percent increase in the corporate profitability index, from 153 to 199 (i.e., $153 \times (1.00 + 0.30) = 153 \times 1.30 = 199$), is illustrative of the next phase of the stock market:

$$DJIA = (199)/(0.10 + 0.06) = (199)/(0.16) = 1244. \qquad (8)$$

These simple (and rough) calculations suggest two points of interest concerning the stock market rally of 1982–3. First, the initial leg of the rally from below 800 to 1000, a 200(-plus)-point move, was mostly the direct response of the stock market to lower interest rates. Second, the indirect response of lower interest rates, leading to a stronger economy and higher corporate profits, was responsible for the next major leg of the bull market, which took the DJIA from the 1000 level in late 1982 to 1250 by the fall of 1983.

The bull market of 1985–6 also was impressive. The Dow Jones Industrial Average climbed from below the 1300 level in the spring of 1985 to over 1900 in the summer of 1986.

This bull market was driven primarily by a dramatic decline in interest rates. From March 1985 through March 1986, long-term US Treasury bond yields fell from 12.00 to 7.50 percent, a fall of 450 basis points, or a 43 percent gain in value for a 12 percent coupon, 20-year bond. This occurred during a period of sluggish economic growth, suggesting expectations of stagnant corporate profits. For our calculations, corporate profits will have grown substantially since 1983 (when our index stood at 199). Thus, the corporate profitability index would have been around 230, reflecting the strength of the 1983–4 economic recovery. With corporate profits at this higher level, but not expected to grow further owing to the sluggish economy, we can estimate (calculate) the direct effect on the stock market from the bond market rally. By this method, the drop in interest rates alone can account for 436 points of the 600(-plus)-point move that actually occurred in the DJIA: from

$$DJIA = (230)/(0.12 + 0.06) = (230)/(0.18) = 1278 \qquad (9)$$

to

$$DJIA = (230)/(0.075 + 0.06) = (230)/(0.135) = 1704 \qquad (10)$$

Again, these calculations are purely suggestive of the notion that interest rate moves can be an extremely powerful force affecting the stock market. There will be various leads and lags present in actual fact, as dividends are paid, as expectations react more or less swiftly to rate changes, and as international factors, such as the exchange rate, affect corporate profitability. The basic principal, however, will still stand. The bond market can drive the stock market and explain large moves in stock prices. And this conclusion is based on a straightforward application of opportunity cost theory – namely, that the relationship between competing investments is critical to understanding how changes in one market affect other markets.

When interest rates fall, investments in the bond market at these lower rates will not earn as much as before. Thus, if other investments are still expected to earn high returns, even after rates have fallen, these alternative investments will find their value rising as investors shift funds toward them. By the same analysis, if interest rates rise, one can get a high return from the bond market. The stock market must improve its offer if it is to hold its value. If investor expectations about corporate profitability remain constant, the stock market will suffer as interest rates rise.

This basic relationship – that falling interest rates are good for the stock market and rising interest rates are bad for it – is derived from the theory of opportunity costs. And it is consistent with the generally observed phenomenon that equity price/earnings (PE) ratios rise when interest rates decline. In the language of Wall Street, a given level of corporate earnings, discounted (valued) using lower and lower interest rates, will yield higher stock valuations.

Also, stock market behavior, as was illustrated in the numerical examples, depends on expectations of corporate profitability. In many cases this may reinforce the direct interest rate effect, but it does not have to reinforce it. For instance, in a recession interest rates often fall, but corporate profits often become losses. The positive effect of falling interest rates may be outweighed by the expectations of corporate losses.

The simple model presented here illustrates both these points; the direct effect of interest rates on the stock market, and the indirect effect which depends on corporate profits. These are powerful conclusions from straightforward concepts.

10

The Shape of Things to Come: The Yield Curve

The *yield curve* represents the yields available on fixed-rate debt instruments of similar credit quality for varying maturities. Figure 10.1 illustrates a yield curve with a positive slope, indicating that interest rates on shorter-term investments are lower than those on longer-term investments. An inverted or negatively sloped yield curve is just the opposite (figure 10.2): interest rates on longer-term investments are lower than those on shorter-term investments.

Yield curves contain a wealth of information concerning market expectations and market risk assessments. Wall Street traders watch the yield curve – its shape, and how it changes – for critical clues concerning the future direction of interest rates generally. Unfortunately, there is no one set of guidelines for decoding the information contained in the yield curve. This chapter makes an effort, however, to provide insights into the strategic portfolio investment clues that yield curves contain.

Basic Shapes

There are two basic shapes for yield curves: (1) positively sloped, or normal, and (2) negatively sloped, or inverted. The shapes illustrated in figures 10.1 and 10.2 are also described in table 10.1, which gives actual yield curve data from several different periods.

The positively sloped yield curve, with interest rates rising as the maturities lengthen, is often referred to as the 'normal' shape of the yield curve. This positive shape does occur frequently, but there can exist extended periods of time in which negative or inverted yield curves are the rule.

Yield curves must be expressed in terms of constant credit risk, to assure that the information they contain is purely a maturity effect.

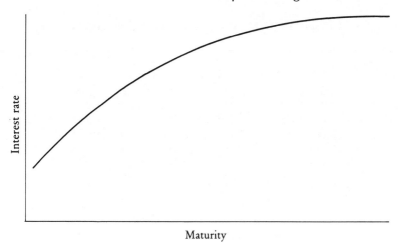

Figure 10.1   Positively sloped or normal yield curve

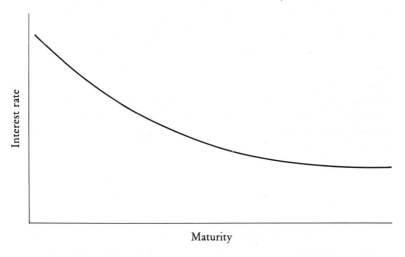

Figure 10.2   Negatively sloped or inverted yield curve

For this reason, all of the yield curves used in this chapter should be considered as the curves for US Treasury, fixed-rate debt securities.

On Wall Street, too, the common pratice is to use the Treasury yield curve as the standard. All other debt securities, such as corporate bonds or mortgage-backed securities, are priced in relation to the US Treasury yield curve. So a 10-year, non-callable, fixed-rate bond issued by a triple-A credit such as IBM would trade on Wall Street at a small, relatively constant increment over the interest rate on 10-year US Treasury securities; a 3-year, fixed-rate

Table 10.1   US Treasury securities yield curves,
1980–1986 (%)

Maturity	Dates			
	3/80	*3/82*	*3/8*	*3/86*
3 months	16.02	13.28	9.88	6.76
6 months	16.47	13.83	10.29	6.89
1 year	15.95	13.98	10.59	7.04
5 years	13.47	13.98	12.02	7.46
10 years	12.75	13.86	12.32	7.78
20 years	12.49	13.75	12.45	8.09

Note There is an inverted yield curve in the March 1980 column, which occurred during a period of very tight monetary policy. In more normal times, such as March 1984 and March 1986, the yield curve reverted to a positive slope. The absolutely lower level of interest rates for March 1986 reflects the dramatic decline in inflation that occurred between the initial periods and this period. March 1982 represents a relatively flat curve.

bond issued by a single-A credit would trade at a larger increment above the 3-year US Treasury interest. The size of the increments above US Treasury interest rates, whether 25 basis points or 150 basis points, is referred to as the *credit spread*, and has nothing to do with the yield curve.

Reading the Yield Curve

The yield curve is nothing if not a wealth of information about market expectations. By explicitly comparing the yields on securities of different maturities, you are getting into the heart of questions involving time and the possible events that may shape interest rates in the future. Not surprisingly, then, theories of the yield curve revolve around various versions of expectations theory – that is, of what expectations are reflected in the yield curve.

In general, there are three expectational issues that the yield curve, in some sense, is attempting to foretell: (1) future interest rates, (2) future inflation, and (3) monetary policy, in terms of how it may change from the current stance. These issues form a hierarchy of analysis which starts with straightforward assumptions about market expectations and then gets more complex rather quickly. We will tackle each of these issues in order. Before we can do that, however, we must examine a theory of the yield curve that does not involve expectations: liquidity.

Liquidity

In the often rather sloppy language of Wall Street, liquidity can take on two different meanings. First, liquidity can be considered the ability to buy or sell a security, in large volume, without moving its price and without paying a large commission or *bid–ask spread*. Second, liquidity is often considered to mean the ability of a security to hold its value as prices in related markets change. These definitions both have implications for the yield curve and for a concept known as the *liquidity premium*.

The liquidity premium is a cost that is generally presumed to grow larger as the maturity of a bond increases. Hence, the existence of a liquidity premium helps to explain the positive slope of normal yield curves.

The liquidity premium arguments are of mixed validity in today's markets. To understand liquidity premiums, the following considerations are important. When you purchase any asset, you must always assess the possibility of selling that asset and the costs that may be incurred at the time of the sale. Conceptually, when a bond is considered liquid, the costs associated with the sale of the bond are low; whereas an illiquid bond will have very high costs at the time of sale.

There are two types of costs affecting the liquidity of an asset, in this case bonds, and they are best described by an example. Suppose you own a large position in the bonds of an unknown company, such as Acme Integrated, Inc. The bonds may have been purchased at the time of original issue for a substantial premium over US Treasuries – the *credit spread*. Now, however, you want to sell the bonds. You call your broker and the response is as follows: Sure, we can buy those bonds from you – at price X (which is an exceptionally low price). The reason for the low price is that the broker knows that by selling these bonds in large quantity the price of the bond will move lower; in other words, the addition of your supply to the market will depress the price. Also, the broker knows that it may take some time and effort to find buyers, and you must pay him for that.

Brokers will often quote simultaneously a price at which they will buy and a price at which they will sell the same bond. The spread between these two prices is the bid-ask spread. The larger it is, the less liquid is the bond and the more it costs the seller to close the bond position.

The preceding example used the bonds of Acme Integrated to make the point of illiquidity because US Treasury bonds of any maturity are now considered extremely liquid in the sense just applied. There was a time, however, when longer-term maturities, even in US Treasury debt, were less liquid than shorter-term maturities, in the specific sense that they were traded at wider bid-ask spreads and that trades in large sizes could move market prices. This is no longer the case. US Treasury securities of all maturities are actively traded, in large size, at narrow bid-ask spreads, without necessarily moving market prices. As a result, one is not likely to pay a premium for liquidity of this type in the Treasury yield curve.

The other concept sometimes associated with liquidity is applicable to the Treasury yield curve. This is the concept of value stability in the face of changing interest rates. Along the yield curve, the arithmetic of interest rate risk is extremely impressive. Suppose you take a $1 million position in four US Treasury securities, all of different maturity. That is, you buy $1 million each of the 3-month Treasury bill, the 6-month Treasury bill, the 10-year Treasury bond, and the 20-year Treasury bond. Suppose, further, that the yield curve was flat at 8 percent when these purchases were made and the 10-and 20-year bonds offered 8 percent coupons. That is, the computed yield to maturity of each of these securities was 8 percent at the time of the purchase. Now suppose that, the day after the purchase, interest rates rise to 10 percent across the yield curve; that is, the flat yield curve moves up from 8 to 10 percent. If you had to value that portfolio before the interest rate move, the initial value would have been $4 million (at 8 percent rates); but the value after the rate rise would be only $3.7 million (at 10 percent rates). The loss in value of each component is strikingly different: 0.5 percent for the 3-month bill, 1.0 percent for the 6-month bill, 13.3 percent for the 10-year bond, and 18.9 percent for the 20-year bond. The decline in the value of the total portfolio was 7.5 percent.

The arithmetic of interest rate risk should be crystal-clear. For a given change in interest rates, the longer maturities contain considerably more price risk. A detailed study of this topic is included in chapter 13 on duration analysis. The point here, however, is a simple one. You always pay for risk, and if interest rate risk rises along the yield curve, you can expect risk premiums to rise along the curve as well. In this sense, yield curves are likely to contain a liquidity premium that results in slightly lower interest rates on shorter-term maturities than on longer-term maturities.

This liquidity premium for value preservation in times of volatile interest rates is thought to explain the tendency of yield curves to take on a slightly positive shape on average over long periods of time. And it is for this reason that the positively shaped yield curve is known as the 'normal' yield curve.

The liquidity premium effect on yield curves, however, is often dwarfed by much more powerful forces. These forces have to do with the expectations of future interest rates that are embodied in the yield curve, and they depend on such things as inflation expectations and monetary policy. It is these expectational forces that drive the big swings in the yield curve, both in terms of its shape and in terms of its general up- or down-movements.

Expectations of Future Interest Rates

In a fundamental sense, the yield curve is reflecting expectations of future interest rates. These expectations, as we will argue later, can be distorted by unusually tight or easy monetary policies. But a positively sloped yield curve generally suggests that interest rates are expected to rise, and a negatively sloped curve suggests that interest rates are expected to fall.

To see how this works, think of two different strategies for investing $1 million over a one-year period. First, you could buy $1 million worth of US Treasury bills of 6-month maturity. At the end of the six months, you would reinvest the funds, plus interest earned, into another 6-month Treasury bill. This is the 'rollover strategy.' A second strategy would be simply to invest in 1-year Treasury bills from the start. The difference between these two strategies is the unknown factor of what the interest rate will be on 6-month Treasury bills in six months when the funds have to be reinvested under the rollover strategy. This is *reinvestment risk*, which the second strategy does not incur.

For the moment, assume that you are willing to take this reinvestment risk without charging a risk premium. In the language of economics, the investor is risk-neutral. This means that you believe that there is an equal chance that the first strategy (the six-month rollover strategy) will yield the same final return as the second strategy. Given this expectation, the interest rate on 6-month Treasury bills that must prevail in six months' time in order for the two strategies to yield equal final total returns can be calculated explicitly.

For instance, if the yield curve is flat at 8 percent, in terms of yield to maturity, a rollover strategy requires an interest rate of 8 percent to prevail in six months for this strategy to earn the same 8 percent return that can be earned by buying a 1-year bill initially. The case of a positively sloped yield curve is more interesting. If initially the 6-month bill is priced to yield 8 percent while the 1-year bill is priced to yield 9 percent, then the only way the rollover strategy can yield a final return of 9 percent and match the second strategy is if the interest rate on 6-month bills in six months' time rises to over 10 percent. (Linear averaging does not quite work because of the compounding of interest, so the actual answer exceeds 10 percent.) In this sense, a positively sloped yield curve embodies expectations of rising interest rates.

By the same analysis, a negatively sloped yield curve embodies expectations of falling interest rates. There is always the choice of investing in the 6-month bill and rolling it over into another 6-month bill, or of investing in the 1-year bill. Assuming risk neutrality (no premium for interest rate risk), the expected interest rate at rollover time must be unambiguously lower than the current 6-month bill rate to make the two strategies equivalent. That is, if 6-month bills initially were priced to yield 10 percent and one-year bills 8 percent, the expected rate on 6-month bills in six months' time would have to be less that 6 percent. Clearly, this is a forecast of declining interest rates.

The theory that a positively sloped yield curve implies expectations of higher interest rates and a negatively sloped yield curve implies expectations of falling interest rates is simple enough. Unfortunately, the theory does not tell us how or why these expectations are formed. And obviously, this is a critical issue.

Inflation Expectations

One of the most important relationships involving interest rates is the association between current interest rates and expected inflation. Furthermore, expected changes in inflation rates, either up or down over time, have implications for the shape of the yield curve.

This basic relationship is known as the 'Fisher equation,' named for the late outstanding economist, Irving Fisher. He postulated that current interest rates should be analyzed in terms of two components, inflation expectations and the real interest rate, as follows:

$$Interest\ rates = inflation\ expectations + the\ real\ rate. \quad (1)$$

The concept of the real interest rate is critical to understanding bond markets; the next chapter is dedicated solely to this topic. For now, we will hold real interest rates constant, although they may not be stable over some time periods.

The Fisher equation (1) clearly implies that, holding real interest rates constant, a rise in inflation expectations is associated with a rise in current interest rates. Extrapolating this to different time periods suggests that inflation expectations play a key role in determining the shape of the yield curve.

If inflation is running at 5 percent but is expected to rise to 7 percent the following year, then, with constant real interest rates of say 3 percent, the one-year interest rates would be 8 percent today and would be expected to rise to 10 percent next year. This would imply a positively sloped yield curve. As in the previous section on expectations, comparing the two strategies of rolling-over short-term securities and buying and holding longer-term securities, one would argue that, if the one-year rate was 8 percent today and was expected to go to 10 percent in one year's time, then the two-year rate today must be about 9 percent.

The implications of this relationship are clear. Expectations of inflation are reflected in current interest rates, and expectations of rising (falling) inflation will be reflected in positively (negatively) sloped yield curves.

The next step is to understand how the market forms expectations of inflation. Unfortunately, this is a subject of intense controversy which has generated numerous books. In this discussion we will focus on only one of the key players in the determination of future inflation; the central bank, or, in the United States, the Federal Reserve Bank.

Monetary Policy and the Yield Curve

By no means is monetary policy the only determinant of future inflation and inflation expectations. But changes in monetary policy *can* have immediate and dramatic effects on the yield curve, depending on whether the central bank is fighting inflation with tight policies or stimulating the economy through lower interest rates and easier policies.

The central bank in the United States – the Federal Reserve Bank, or 'Fed' – conducts monetary policy predominantly by buying and selling Treasury securities, known as *open-market operations*. These operations alter the financial conditions in the money markets. For the most part, Fed open-market operations directly affect short-term interest rates, and in particular the short-term interest rate known as the *'Federal funds rate.'* This is the interest rate that commercial banks use to trade their excess bank reserves. It is the key rate for watching monetary policy in the United States, as other short-term rates take their cues from it. For our purposes, the point is that Fed operations can directly affect short-term interest rates.

The power that the Fed has to affect short-term interest rates is impressive and can be very dramatic. For instance, in June 1980 the Fed was strictly following its targets aimed at reducing the growth rate of the money stock to reduce inflation. At that time inflation was in the double-digit range, but the recent imposition of credit controls had reduced the growth of the money supply sharply and interest rates had fallen rapidly. The yield curve ran from 7.30 percent on 3-month bills to 9.80 percent on 20-year bonds, a positively sloped curve. By December 1980, the 3-month bill was yielding 16.35 percent and the 20-year bond was yielding 12.49 percent. Not only had interest rates risen sharply, but the yield curve had shifted to an inverted shape. What had happened? The money supply had begun to grow rapidly again in the second half of the year after credit restrictions were removed, and the Fed had aggressively tightened short-term money market conditions in attempts to reduce the money growth.

To take this example further, by 1982 the yield curve had taken on a slightly positive slope. The economy was in a recession, and the Fed finally moved to ease policy. The yield curve dropped across the board and shifted to a more positive slope. That is, from February 1982 to October 1982, the 3-month bill went from 14.15 to 8.00 percent, while the 20-year bond went from 14.50 to 11.00 percent. Not only did short-term rates drop 615 basis points in this eight-month period, but the spread between the 3-month bill and the 20-year bond went from a modest 35 basis points to a large 300 basis points. Movements like these have spawned an industry known as 'Fed-watching,' for, clearly, over some time periods the Fed can dominate movements in the yield curve.

The Fed's actions are not inconsistent with the relationship of inflation expectations to the yield curve. When monetary policy is aggressively tightened, the yield curve shifts from a very positive slope to a flat or even inverted shape. Inverted yield curves are consistent with expectations that inflation will fall in the future. That is, because of the tight policy, inflation expectations are lower for the coming years than they are for the current period.

By the same token, a very easy monetary policy is often associated with expectations of rising inflation. In turn, these expections of rising inflation translate into a positively sloped yield curve.

There is, however, much more to monetary policy's effects on interest rates, because monetary policy appears able to alter real interest rates over certain time periods. This power complicates the effects on both the level of interest rates and the yield curve, and it is the topic of discussion in the next chapter.

Summary

Basically, the yield curve embodies some risk premium for liquidity, in the sense of the arithmetic of interest rate risk. For a given capital value, longer-term maturities involve more interest rate risk than shorter-term maturities. For risk-averse investors, this risk has a price which results in securities of longer-term maturities paying slightly more interest than short-term securities. The result is a modestly positively sloped yield curve, known as a normal yield curve.

The big swings in interest rates and changes in the shape of the yield curve come from changes in expectations. Here, there is a hierarchy of complexity. At the basic level, the yield curve embodies an expectation of future interest rates. For example, positively sloped yield curves are associated with expectations of rising rates. This, however, does not tell how these interest rate expectations were formed.

The next level of complexity argues that inflation expectations are one, but only one, of the keys to understanding how the market forms interest rate expectations. This leads into territory that is well beyond the scope of this book, namely, inflation theory. But one area of the inflation process – the role of monetary policy – is too important not to mention. At this level of complexity, the point to note is that unusually tight monetary policies result in inverted yield curves, while loose policies are associated with positively sloped yield curves.

11

Separating Reality from Illusion:
Real Interest Rates

Real interest rates are not a complex concept. They are just the difference between the current interest rate and the expected rate of inflation. But real interest rates are controversial, because high real interest rates will supposedly depress economic growth, slowing inflation and causing unemployment. More or less, this happened in the 1980–2 period, but 1983 saw the first postwar economic recovery begin in grand style with no relief from high real interest rates.

Questions have then arisen as to what role real interest rates actually play in determining economic growth and future inflation. Furthermore, some analysts have even gone so far as to argue that real interest rates have not been as high as many have supposed. They are being measured incorrectly.

In this chapter, real interest rates will be investigated from a variety of viewpoints. What do real interest rates really mean? How should they be measured? What are the differences between the short-term and long-term economic effect of relatively high real interest rates?

Real Interest Rates Are Forward-looking

Interest rates reflect the opportunity cost of lending money for a specified period of time. Over the period during which the money is being lent, several things can happen.

An earlier version of this chapter was originally published by Stern, Stewart and Company in their newsletter, 'Free Cash Flow'.

First, inflation can eat away the real value of the money. That is, when the money is repaid, it will no longer buy the same amount of goods (e.g., TV sets, gold, food, etc.) than it did on the day it was lent. Obviously, the lender must be compensated for an expected decrease in the purchasing power of money, and the borrower is compensated both by getting the use of the money before inflation depreciates its value and by repaying the debt in depreciated money.

Second, the lender could do other things with the money if he did not lend it. The lender could choose from a selection of alternative financial investments, buy real estate, consume more, etc. Foregoing these alternatives has its price, and that price is captured in the real interest rate.

More correctly, it is the *expected* real interest rate. During the period of the loan, inflation may not depreciate the value of the money at the anticipated rate, or the loan may not be repaid on time (or at all): these are risks that lenders take. They expect to earn a real return for taking these risks. But the actual real return that is earned cannot be computed until the loan is repaid. Interest rates *today* do not reflect the actual real return that will be earned *tomorrow*. Interest rates reflect only the *expected* real return.

In equation form, the interest rate can be divided into two components, expected inflation and expected real return:

Nominal interest rate = expected inflation + expected real return.

Interest rates are forward-looking. They anticipate future inflation, which erodes the purchasing power of money, and they anticipate the real return that must be earned to compensate the lender for the risk being taken and the opportunities being foregone.

Measuring the Real Interest Rate

The fact that real interest rates are forward-looking is a major problem when one tries to measure them. The nominal interest rate can be observed; that part is easy. But the expected inflation rate is not reported in the *Wall Street Journal* or anywhere else – and neither is the expected real return.

Looking Backwards

Many analysts, when faced with this lack of observable data on forward-looking variables, inflationary expectations, and the expected real return, decide to look backwards. They take last year's inflation rate and substract that from today's interest rate. The result is their estimate of today's real interest rate. But is it a good estimate?

This *ex post* method assumes that last year's inflation rate is a good predictor of inflationary expectations. In the 1950s, and even into the early 1960s, there was some evidence that this method was adequate, simply because inflation rates were low and stable. It did not matter. But in the 1970s and 1980s annual inflation rates were much higher and considerably more variable. Last year's inflation rate is a good predictor of future inflation only if the inflation rate is steady, which it no longer is. Many analysts, however, when they speak of high real interest rates, are speaking of real interest rates measured in this *ex post* fashion. (See figure 11.1)

Assume Away the Problem

To measure the real interest rate that matters – the expected or *ex ante* real interest rate – requires a forward-looking view of inflationary expectations or, more directly, a forward-looking view of expected real returns. There are several competing methods that are forward-looking, but they still have their drawbacks.

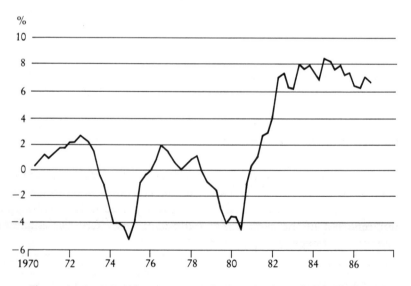

Figure 11.1   US real interest rates: looking backward, 1970–86 (US Treasury bond yield minus percentage change in consumer price index)

One procedure, interestingly enough, is to assume that the expected real interest rate never changes. If one makes this assumption, then the current nominal interest rate can be used to estimate the market's forecast of future inflation. That is, if interest rates are 12 percent and the real interest rate is permanently held at 3 percent, then inflationary expectations are 9 percent.

As a group, monetarists tend to lean toward this method. It allows them to focus on inflationary expectations – their problem of choice – rather than on real interest rates. But they do have their reasons, and they are grounded in a long-run view of how real interest rates are determined, which will be discussed later.

Looking Forward

Another, rather interesting, method is to invent a marketable security that explicitly eliminates inflation risk. In this case, the borrower must repay money that can purchase the same amount of real stuff as when the money was borrowed. There is an inflation adjustment made that compensates the lender for any inflation. If this is done, then the interest rate on such a security should reflect only the expected real return, and furthermore, that real return should be free of inflation risk (i.e., the risk that the inflation forecast implicit in nominal interest rates will be wrong).

There is such a security. The United Kingdom has issued a debt instrument which is adjusted in accordance with the published retail price index. To measure the expected real interest rate, all one needs to do is to look at the interest rate on these securities. By this method, sterling real rates have been quite stable in the 2–3 percent range for the past several years.

Of course, taking the sterling real rate as a good estimate of the US dollar real interest rate may be a leap of faith for some. But if market participants efficiently seek the highest expected real returns anywhere in the world, and there is plenty of evidence that they do, then applying UK real rates to the United States may be justified. However, we will return to this measure of real rates later.

Conceptually Speaking

Setting aside the measurement issue, a number of theories exist concerning how real interest rates are set. The short-run theories depend primarily on monetary and fiscal policy to move real interest rates.

Long-run theories are based on an historical perspective of the real growth rate of the economy and efficiency of new investments. More recent theories take a middle ground, and focus on the risks being priced by the expected real interest rate. These latter theories appear to hold much promise, and in part reconcile the different results one gets from using the different methods to measure real interest rates.

Short-run Theories

Short-run views of what causes high real interest rates focus either on fiscal policy or on monetary policy. From the fiscal side, the culprit is the federal deficit, which supposedly 'crowds-out' private investment, driving interest rates higher. On the monetary side, the Federal Reserve is presumed to have the power to force short-term interest rates higher as part of its powers to 'tighten' credit.

Neither of these mechanisms should cause real interest rates to stay high for long periods of time. If fiscal policy continues to crowd private investment from the market, then the economy moves to a slower long-term real growth path and real interest rates eventually decline. If monetary policy remains 'tight' for too long, a recession is induced, which also brings real and nominal interest rates down.

Long-run Theories

In the long run, real interest rates are linked to real economic growth. Real interest rates, *ex post*, measure the additional amount of wealth that the economy has created and that is available for distribution as a return on investment. Over a period of a few years, wealth could decline (recession) and real interest rates could stay high. But over longer periods, if the economy is not growing, then high real interest rates cannot be sustained. There is simply no incremental income to pay the high real rates.

From an investment perspective, this means that the efficiency of new investment in generating wealth (the marginal efficiency of capital, as academics might say) must be closely associated with the long-term real growth potential of the economy. If the United States is perceived to have a long-run real growth potential of 3–4 percent then real interest rates should not deviate from that range for sustained periods of time.

These long-run concepts are what lie behind the. general

presumption made by monetarists that the real interest rate is relatively stable over time.

New Approaches

A new approach to analyzing real interest rates focuses on the opportunity costs and the risks associated with lending funds. The opportunity cost is the foregone investment, or what else one could have done with the money, and some base real return is expected here. There are essentially two types of risk: inflation forecast risk, and credit risk. Credit risk is the traditional one, and measures the chance that the loan will not be repaid in full or in part. The higher the chance of such an occurrence, the higher the compensation for taking such a risk.

The new approach focuses on inflation forecast risk. If you expect the purchasing power of your money to depreciate by 10 percent over the course of a one year loan, then you would want an additional 10 percent interest to cover the loss of real purchasing power. Suppose that the 10 percent inflation forecast is wrong, and that inflation actually runs at a 15 percent pace. The risk of this occurrence must be priced into the real interest rate, in addition to the standard charge for credit risk. (See Brad Cornell's 'The Future of Floating Rate Bonds,' in *The Revolution in Corporate Finance* Basil Blackwell, (1986).

During the 1950s and 1960s, the variance in the inflation rate from year to year was minimal. Even if one took the previous year's inflation rate as the best guess of next year's rate, the chance of being very wrong was very low. This was not the case in the 1970s and the 1980s, when inflation rates, year to year, were bouncing all around. Perhaps this inflation forecast risk is keeping real interest rates higher longer than is usually thought possible.

Also, the existence of an inflation forecast risk premium would change the analysis of the UK securities, which are indexed on the inflation rate. With no inflation forecast required in these securities, there would be no inflation forecast risk premium. So the real rate on these securities would be unambiguously lower than on non-indexed securities. Countries with more variable and unpredictable inflation rates would have higher real rates than countries with stable inflation, other things being equal.

Confused?

If real interest rates are still confusing after reading this discussion, then join the club. There is no consensus among economists on this issue, except that it is very critical for economic policy and for economic forecasting, and very important that the issue receive further study.

12

Coping with Maturity:
Duration Analysis

One of the more interesting areas of change sweeping Wall Street over the last decade has been the rise of the academic researcher. In the 1960s, PhDs were largely banished to their ivory towers and received little or no respect from Wall Street. More recently, however, academic scholars have made major contributions to portfolio risk management. These contributions have been recognized by Wall Street in many ways, but the most obvious is the actual employment of teams of former academics in think-tank shops directed toward developing portfolio risk management products.

In the area of interest rate risk management, the use of duration analysis provides a classic example of the rise of the academic on Wall Street. Other areas, such as options analysis, have also seen a major invasion by top-quality scholars.

In this chapter we will attempt to take duration analysis down from its lofty academic heights and demonstrate why the concept has captured Wall Street's attention as an important tool in the management of interest rate risk. We will begin by defining the concept and offering basic examples of its usefulness. Then we will illustrate how the duration measure is calculated. Finally, the applications of duration analysis and some of its problems will be highlighted.

Measuring Interest Rate Risk

In an era of highly volatile interest rates, portfolio managers and investors have very strong incentives to understand the sensitivity of their fixed-income assets and liabilities to changes in interest rates. The concept of *duration* is very useful in this regard because it can measure how much the value of a fixed-income instrument or portfolio will change for a given change in interest rates.

For example, a bond with a duration index of 20 years is more value-sensitive than a bond with a duration index of 10 years. That is, across the yield curve, if interest rates fall by 100 basis points or a full percentage point, the bond with the longer duration will see its value rise by more than any bond with a shorter duration. Conversely, if interest rates rise, long-duration bonds will lose more in value than shorter-duration bonds. Duration summarizes in one number, expressed in years, the value sensitivity of any fixed-income instrument or portfolio to changes in interest rates.

Maturity versus Duration

Maturity is the traditional measure that competes with duration as a method of ranking the price sensitivity of fixed-income instruments. The value of longer-maturity bonds is generally considered more sensitive to interest rate changes than that of shorter-maturity bonds. In an era of plain vanilla bonds and only small changes in interest rates, such as the 1950s and 1960s, this concept worked well enough. In the highly volatile 1970s and 1980s, and in an era of floating-rate bonds, zero-coupon bonds, and other instruments with various whistles and bells attached, maturity can be a very misleading measure of interest rate risk. And when the risks are high, the costs and potential investment mistakes associated with a misleading measure can be very large.

The problem of using maturity as a measure of interest rate risk can be seen in two examples. These are summarized in table 12.1.

First, observe that a 5-year bond with an 8 percent fixed-rate coupon for the life of the bond will have a very different sensitivity to interest rate changes than a 5-year floating-rate bond, where the interest rate is reset every three months based on currently prevailing short-term interest rates. The fixed-rate bond will have substantial price sensitivity to interest rate change, while the floating-rate bond will have a value very close to its principal (face) value regardless of interest rate changes.

Next, compare two 20-year maturity, fixed-rate bonds. One has a coupon of 10 percent, and the other a coupon of 0 percent; that is, it is a *zero-coupon bond.* The maturity, obviously, is the same. If interest rates rise from 8 to 10 percent, however, the value of the zero-coupon bond will fall by much more than the value of the 10

Table 12.1 Interest rate risk and maturity

	Value of a $1000 bond under different interest rates[a]		
	8%	10%	12%
5-year floating rate[b]	$1000	$1000	$1000
5-year 10% fixed rate[c]	1076	1000	930
20-year 10% fixed rate[d]	1184	1000	856
20-year zero-coupon[e]	215	149	104

[a] All calculations are made on the assumption of a flat yield curve at the current rate given at the top of the column. That is, interest rates are the same for all maturities, including 3-month, 5-year, and 20-year. All interest rates are assumed to move up and down together.

[b] 5-year maturity, interest rate reset every six months at the current interest rate, and paid semi-annually.

[c] 5-year maturity, interest rate equal to 10% for the life of the bond and paid semi-annually.

[d] 20-year maturity, interest rate equal to 10% for the life of the bond and paid semi-annually.

[e] 20-year maturity, the bond pays no interest.

percent coupon bond. Conversely, if interest rates were to fall, the capital gains would be much larger on the zero-coupon bond than on the 10 percent coupon bond.

In both of these examples, the maturities of the two bonds being compared are identical. A given change in interest rates, however, produces very different effects on the value of the two bonds. Clearly, a knowledge of the maturity of two different bonds is not enough information to determine the interest rate risk inherent in each bond. You must also take into account the structure of interest payments, such as fixed or floating rate, the size of coupon, etc. The duration measure accomplishes this, while the maturity measure does not. In essence, duration is a measure that has been developed to overcome the problems associated with trying to compare the interest rate risk of bonds with similar maturities but different coupons.

Principal Risk versus Reinvestment Risk

The basic problem with using maturity as a measure of interest rate risk is that it does not separate principal risk (or *price risk*) from reinvestment risk. These two risks work in opposite directions, but may not exactly offset each other.

Principal risk is the risk that a bond's price will rise or fall in value if interest rates change. If interest rates rise, bond values fall, because the stream of interest payments due the bondholder is discounted at a higher interest rate. Consequently, the present value of the bond has been reduced, since it is being depreciated (higher interest rates) faster. How much a bond's value will rise (or fall) for a given fall (or rise) in interest rates will depend on reinvestment risk and the bond's coupon.

Reinvestment risk is the risk that the interest payments received from the bond will be reinvested at current interest rates which are different from the bond's coupon rate, and from one interest payment period to the next. Bond yields are traditionally calculated and quoted by making the assumption that coupon payments are reinvested at prevailing rates. Interest rates, however, can and do change, and these changes will effect the realized return on the bond.

To provide an example, suppose you invest in a 20-year fixed-rate bond with a 10 percent coupon rate while current interest rates are 10 percent across all maturities. Under this scenario, each interest payment received can be reinvested at 10 percent. If interest rates fall to 8 percent, then interest payments can be reinvested only at 8 percent. This will lower the total return of the bond. That is, as interest rates fall (rise), income from reinvesting interest payments falls (rises). This factor must be taken into account when valuing a bond.

Zero-coupon Bonds

Unlike coupon-paying bonds, zero-coupon bonds have no reinvestment risk. When purchasing a zero-coupon bond, one knows with certainty what the total return on the bond will be if it is held to maturity. Since there will be only one payment, namely, the redemption of the bond at face value upon maturity, price risk is the only consideration.

To value a zero-coupon bond, one uses prevailing interest rates to discount the value of the principal that will be received at redemption. This substantially reduces the value of the bond today, since the final and only payment may be years away. Therefore, zero-coupon bonds are sold at very deep discounts, and are also known as 'deep-discount bonds.' Note, however, that deep-discount bonds also include bonds with very low, but non-zero, coupons.

Several characteristics of zero-coupon bonds deserve attention. First, they have no reinvestment risk. Second, the bonds are valued at a substantial discount from face value. This discount is higher when interest rates are higher. And finally, the price risk of zero-coupon bonds increases as the maturity increases.

This final point is critical to understanding duration analysis. Unambiguously, the longer the maturity of a zero-coupon bond, the greater the price risk. This can be seen in table 12.2, which shows the value of 5-, 10-, and 20-year zero-coupon bonds for a given set of interest rates. As the maturity lengthens, the difference in bond value between a low interest rate environment and a high interest rate environment increases. For example, if interest rates start at 8 percent, a $1000, 5-year, zero-coupon bond is worth $681, while a 20-year bond is worth $215. A 200-basis-point increase in interest rates to 10 percent will decrease the value of the 5-year bond by $60 per $1000 bond, or 8.8 percent, while the value of a 20-year bond will fall by $66, or 30.7 percent.

Table 12.2   Value of a $1000 zero-coupon bond as interest rates change

| Maturity | Current interest rates | | | | | % change in value as rates go from 8% to 6% |
	2%	4%	6%	8%	10%	
5 years	906	822	747	681	621	9.7
10 years	820	675	558	463	386	10.5
20 years	673	456	312	215	149	45.1
30 years	552	308	174	99	57	75.8

In the case of zero-coupon bonds, and only zero-coupon bonds, maturity is an unambiguous index of the price sensitivity to changes in interest rates. That is, if zero-coupon bonds are ranked by maturity from the shortest to the longest, the bonds with the longest maturity will have the greatest price risk. The lack of ambiguity in this ranking by maturity is due to the absence of reinvestment risk.

Calculating Duration

Duration can be calculated for any bond by reducing it to zero-coupon bond equivalence. This is accomplished by treating each coupon payment from the bond as a separate zero-coupon bond. These payments are valued as individual zero-coupon bonds, as is the final payment of principal. Then, the maturity of each part is weighted by its relative value to the total value of the bond. The sum of the maturities of the parts times this weighting yields the duration for the whole bond.

Thus, duration is the price-weighted maturity of a bond. What is being measured is the amount of time that must pass before the reinvestment effects of changes in interest rates offset the value or principal risk from interest rate changes. Remember, that these risks – reinvestment risk and principal risk – work in opposite directions. These considerations make the duration of a coupon-paying bond a measurement that is expressed in time increments (years), just like maturity.

Notice that, since zero-coupon bonds have no reinvestment risk, it takes the whole maturity of the bond before the principal risk goes to zero and can be (theoretically) offset by the zero reinvestment risk. This makes the duration of a zero-coupon bond equal to its maturity.

Table 12.3 is an example of the calculation of a 7 percent coupon, 5-year bond when interest rates were 10 percent. Notice that each semi-annual interest payment is treated as a separate zero-coupon bond. The final calculation gives a duration for this bond of 2.747 years. This means that the interest rate sensitivity of this bond is exactly the same as a zero-coupon bond of 2.747 years' maturity.

If these calculations were performed on a zero-coupon bond, the duration would equal its maturity. There would be only one payment to value, which would occur at maturity and would get a weight of 100 percent. Notice that the duration of a zero-coupon bond is always equal to its maturity, while the duration of a coupon-paying bond will always be less than its maturity.

Problems

Unfortunately, duration does not provide a perfect measure of interest rate risk. Calculating duration involves a number of

Table 12.3   Calculating the duration of a $100 face value bond, paying a 7% coupon, priced to give a 10% yield to maturity

Cash inflow Date (yrs)	Cash inflow amount ($)	Cash inflows discounted at 10% ($)	Price weights	Price-weighted maturities (yrs)
0.5	3.50	3.34[a]	0.036[c]	0.018[d]
1.0	3.50	3.18	0.034	0.034
1.5	3.50	3.03	0.033	0.050
2.0	3.50	2.89	0.031	0.062
2.5	3.50	2.76	0.030	0.075
3.0	103.50	77.76	0.836	2.508
		92.96[b]	1.000	2.747[e]
		(current price)		(duration)

[a] $3.50/(1.10)^{0.5}$
[b] Current price sums all cash inflows discounted by the yield to maturity (10%).
[c] $3.34/$92.96.
[d] 0.036×0.5 yrs.
[e] Duration is the sum of all price-weighted maturities.

Source: 'Uses of Duration Analysis for the Control of Interest Rate Risk,' by Alden Toevs, Morgan Stanley & Company, New York, 1984.

assumptions about interest rates and yield curves that have been overlooked in the preceding sections. These assumptions cause two problems that are worthy of note: yield curve shifts and duration drift. There are other technical issues as well, but the problems are not insurmountable. The informed user, however, should be aware of the potential trouble spots.

The most straightforward method of calculating duration is to assume that the yield curve retains the same shape over the life of the bond. The curve can shift up or down as interest rates move, but it must not change shape. As anyone who observes interest rates knows, this assumption is constantly violated. This assumption does simplify the mathematics, though.

What has to be assessed is the cost of such a simplifying assumption. Extensive research has indicated that the costs are not very high, unless the yield curve shifts are huge. If they are, then durations must be recalculated and the portfolio adjusted accordingly. As will be seen, duration needs to be recalculated regularly anyway, so this cost is relatively small. And there exist significantly more complex formulas for calculating duration which attempt to reduce these problems.

The second problem area is duration drift. This term refers to the fact that, even without an interest rate change, regular adjustments are required to maintain a specific duration. As an example, consider the fact that a coupon-paying bond with a duration of five years today will not have a duration of exactly four years in one year's time. Small adjustments, therefore, are periodically necessary to counter duration drift.

Other problem areas also create the need for minor adjustments or portfolio rebalancing. Periodic coupon payments have to be invested. Corrections for small discrepancies in the duration calculation owing to changes in the shape of the yield curve have to be made. This implies that, in order to keep a portfolio of bonds at a specific duration, periodically some bonds of varying maturities will need to be bought and others sold.

Fortunately, neither duration drift nor the errors from yield curve shifts is considered by practitioners to constitute an unsolvable problem. Indeed, both are considered quite manageable, predominantly by making regular recalculations of duration measures and taking actions, usually small, to rebalance the portfolio so as to regain the desired duration.

Applications

Duration analysis has some extremely powerful applications in the area of interest rate risk management. The two that will be highlighted here are asset/liability management and bond portfolio immunization.

Asset/Liability Management

Banks, insurance companies, brokerage houses, and most financial businesses take on extensive liabilities to fund a portfolio of assets. Interest rate risk thus arises from two sources, the assets and the liabilities. There will be times when financial institutions will actively desire to bear some interest rate risk. Being fully hedged is both boring and, being less risky, not as remunerative. Even so, it is essential to be able to quantify the risks being taken, particularly in a volatile interest rate environment.

Duration is a key measure in assessing the mix of interest rate risk in what has become known as asset/liability management. Because the duration measure can be averaged (weighted for value in the portfolio) across different debt instruments, it is an excellent way to summarize, in one measure, the interest rate risk characteristics of an entire portoflio of assets or liabilities. This means that two duration measures can be calculated, one for the liabilities and one for the assets. To the extent that these numbers differ, there exists a duration gap. From these calculations one can determine if the interest rate sensitivity of the liabilities is equal, greater than, or less than the interest rate sensitivity of the assets.

As noted earlier, financial firms may actively desire to mismatch the interest rate sensitivity of assets and liabilities expressly for the purpose of betting that interest rates will go in a certain direction. For example, a bank that thought interest rates were going to decline would desire a very short duration for its liabilities and a longer duration for its assets. If interest rates did decline, the gain in the value of the assets (more interest-rate-sensitive) would be larger than the change in the value from the liabilities (less interest-rate-sensitive).

In the United States in the 1970s, most savings and loan institutions had this duration characteristic. That is, they were borrowing funds (liabilities) of short duration, usually less than one year, and lending funds (assets) for longer terms – as much as 30 years in the case of home mortgages. The duration of the asset portfolio was substantially longer than the duration of the liability portfolio. If interest rates had fallen, these institutions would have made a bundle of money. But in the late 1970s and into the early 1980s, interest rates rose, and many of these firms lost this bet and as a result went bankrupt or were merged with stronger institutions.

Immunization

Interest rate risk poses some special problems for insurance companies and pension funds. They have obligations to pay certain sums of money at specified times in the future, such as on a worker's retirement. To meet these obligations, funds must be invested today so that the money, in specific quantities, will be available when it is needed.

For example, say that an insurance company needs to construct a portfolio to produce $100 million in ten years in order to meet certain obligations that are expected, with a high degree of certainty, to come due at that time. How much money has to be invested today to grow to $100 million in ten years?

One solution would be to buy $100 million worth of ten-year

bonds. Since most bonds pay a coupon every six months, however, this strategy could run into problems if interest rates were to fall and the coupons would have to be reinvested at lower yields. This is the classic reinvestment problem noted earlier.

A second solution would be to buy a portfolio of zero-coupon bonds with ten-year maturities. This portfolio would comprise zero-coupon bonds having a face value of $100 million, purchased at a substantial discount. The discount would depend on the prevailing level of interest rates. This strategy will work, since the portfolio has been immunized from reinvestment risk. Furthermore, the principal risk is acceptable, because the buyer of the bonds fully expects to hold them to maturity. At that time they will be redeemed at par and used to meet the anticipated obligations.

Unfortunately, the quantity of zero coupon bonds available in exactly the maturity needed and with the credit quality desired may be insufficient. This strategy, however, can then be modified by buying a portfolio of bonds of varying coupons and maturities (and credit quality, if this yield and risk is desired). The key is to combine the bonds in such a way as to achieve an average duration of ten years. Such a portfolio is equivalent to an all zero-coupon, 10-year bond portfolio. The portfolio has again been immunized from reinvestment risk. Remember, though, the portfolio manager will have to monitor this portfolio regularly and make small adjustments, known as 'rebalancing,' to correct for such problems as duration drift and coupon reinvestment.

The major disadvantage of immunization is that it is useful only when both the quantity and the timing of future obligations are known with reasonable certainty. If they are not known, then the principal risk associated with a long-duration portfolio may make it an improper investment strategy. In this case, the uncertainty of timing becomes a form of reinvestment risk, which is still being incurred.

Conclusion

In these volatile times, knowing the interest rate risk inherent in bonds with different maturities and coupons is absolutely critical to the management of a bond portfolio. Duration is proving to be far superior to maturity for analyzing and comparing portfolios. As such, duration analysis has become an essential element in the process of managing interest rate risk. Applications go well beyond the examples covered here. Indeed, the analysis of any portfolio that is affected by interest rate shifts can potentially benefit from using duration concepts.

13

Join the Debtors Club: Bond Issuers

The US credit market is truly huge. In 1985, for example, domestic entities, including individuals, corporations, state and local governments, and the federal government, combined to borrow almost $860 billion, as is illustrated in table 13.1. And while the discussion of bond markets or fixed-income debt instruments tends to focus on interest rates, yield curves, and related topics, there are tremendous differences that exist among the various types of bonds available in the markets. This chapter focuses on the different issuers, providing descriptive information about the size and growth of the markets.

Table 13.1 Funds raised in US credit markets in 1985

Net domestic borrowing by sector[a]	$b 1985	% share of market
US government	223.6	26.0
Tax-exempt obligations	152.4	17.7
Corporate bonds	73.9	8.6
Mortgages	236.2	27.5
Consumer credit	96.6	11.2
Bank loans	37.6	4.4
Open market paper[b]	14.6	1.7
Other domestic	24.3	2.8
Total	859.2	100.0

[a] Does not include borrowings in the US credit markets by foreigners.
[b] Includes commercial paper issuance among other types of short-term marketable paper.

Source: *Federal Reserve Bulletin*, table 1.57, January 1987.

The US fixed-income debt market can be divided into five categories: US government and agencies, corporations, state and local governments, foreign entities, and homeowners (through the use of mortgage-backed securities). In addition to these, the US debt market is closely linked to bond markets around the world. US brokerage firms, as well as all international brokers, make markets for their domestic and international clients both in *Eurobonds* of various currencies and in the domestic bond markets of most industrialized countries. Since the emphasis of this book is on Wall Street and US markets, we will focus on the five categories listed initially. Nevertheless, we must always remember that international bond markets represent additional choices for investors in the United States, just as the US markets are open to international investors. In this sense, the discussions here are incomplete.

US Treasury Securities

The US Treasury debt market is the largest and most liquid fixed-income market in the world. By the end of 1986, the debt of the US Treasury will exceed $2 trillion. This debt is held in various forms, including marketable and non-marketable securities. The holders of the debt include US citizens, corporations, foreign governments, and foreign private corporations and individuals. Table 13.2 shows the breakdown of the owners of US Treasury securities, and it is clear that there are a lot of people and institutions assisting in the financing of current and past US budget deficits.

US Treasury securities are considered free of any credit or default risk. The simple reason for this is that the United States issues virtually all of its debt in US dollars and the government has a printing press. Ultimately, any governmental financial crisis could be solved by printing money, which would lead to rising inflation and currency depreciation on the foreign exchange markets; but the holders of US Treasury debt would be repaid in full in newly minted dollars. In this sense, the interest rates on US debt are most closely related to inflation prospects and developments in real interest rates, but are not related to credit considerations.

The US government issues debt in a wide variety of maturities, from 3-month bills to 30-year bonds. This is accomplished through auctions, held weekly for short-term bills and monthly and quarterly for longer-term bonds. The auction method for selling debt means that the US Treasury, through its agent, the Federal

Table 13.2   Public debt of the US Treasury by owner, in 1985

Owner of debt	$b	% share
US government agencies and trust funds	348.9	17.9
Federal Reserve banks	181.3	9.3
Commercial banks	192.2	9.9
Money market funds	25.1	1.3
Insurance companies	93.2	4.8
Other companies	59.0	3.0
Individuals	154.8	8.0
Foreign and international	214.6	11.0
Other[a]	676.8	34.8
Total	1,945.9	100.0

[a] Includes state and local governments, savings and loan institutions, corporate pension trust funds, and dealers and brokers, among others

Source: Federal Reserve Bulletin, table 1.41, January 1987.

Reserve, accepts bids on the debt and sets the interest rate based on the bids received. This has proven to be an extremely efficient mechanism for issuing huge quantities of debt.

Corporations

Corporations use bonds as part of their financial structure, which involves equity, bank lines of credit, leasing arrangements, short-term commercial paper, and a variety of less used privately placed debt instruments. As can be seen in table 13.1, in 1985 net corporate borrowing through the bond market accounted for only 8.6 percent of the total US domestic credit market activity and amounted to only one-third the debt appetite of the US Treasury.

Corporate debt comes in standard fixed-income securities and in debt instruments with numerous whistles and bells, such as with warrants attached, call provisions, equity conversion options, etc. These innovations add to the complexity of the market and make it difficult to compare one bond directly with another.

Credit quality also distinguishes one corporate bond issuer from another. The market's assessment of the ability of a corporation to honor its commitments determines the spread over the US Treasury yield curve at which a given corporation's bonds will trade. Rating agencies, such as Standard & Poors or Moody's, provide credit analysis, and many brokerage houses do so as well. Quite obviously, better credits will trade at smaller premiums over US Treasuries than riskier credits. Table 13.3 gives an example of the effects of credit quality on corporate bond interest rates prevailing in the markets at the end of 1985.

The bonds issued by credits of the least quality have become referred to as 'junk bonds'. Junk bonds, also known more discreetly as 'high-yield bonds,' come from two very different categories of corporations. One such category is the 'fallen star,' that is, a formerly excellent-quality credit that has flirted with financial disaster and now has outstanding bonds that trade at much larger spreads than when they were issued. An example would be the bonds of Chrysler Corporation in the early 1980s. (This company, of course, has successfully returned to profitability, and its bond yields now reflect this improvement in credit quality.) The other category is that of a healthy corporation taking on substantial debt, either to restructure its own balance sheet to take much greater advantage of the tax deductibility of interest or to expand into new areas through large acquisition programs.

The essential characteristic of junk bonds is that their prices and interest rates fluctuate more on the basis of developments in credit quality than in general movements in interest rates. This is to say, the spreads at which they trade relative to US Treasuries can be quite variable as the issuing companies do better or worse.

Table 13.3   Credit quality and interest rate spreads, end 1985

Credit rating	Yield (%) (Dec. 1985)	Spread over US Treasuries (basis pts)
AAA	10.16	66
AA	10.63	113
A	11.19	160
Baa	11.58	208
US Treasures[a]	9.50	

[a] This comparison is based on 12- to 15-year US Treasuries and is only meant to provide a rough benchmark. Various differences in corporate bonds, including call provisions, sinking funds, maturity, etc., will affect how a given credit will trade relative to the US Treasury yield curve.

Source: *Federal Reserve Bulletin*, table 1.35, January 1987

State and Local Governments

Municipal bonds – those debt obligations issued by state and local governments and their agencies – exist as a separate category by courtesy of the US federal tax code. Interest paid on these bonds is not subject to federal tax, unlike the interest of US Treasury debt or on regular corporate debt. These bonds form the tax-exempt obligation category and accounted for 8.7 percent of the debt raised in the US credit markets in 1984 and 17.7 percent in 1985, as many municipalities rushed to market ahead of the tax reform act.

Tax-free status, of course, makes all the difference in the world. Before the passage of the 1986 Tax Reform Act, the top tax bracket was 50 percent. This meant that a federal taxpayer in the 50 percent tax bracket would pay one-half of every additional dollar of interest earned on a bond to the US government. Given this tax bite, tax-exempt municipal bonds can look very attractive. For this reason, such bonds tend to pay lower interest rates than US Treasury debt of similar maturities.

With the passage of the 1986 Tax Reform Act, the marginal tax rate can be 33, 28 or 15 percent, depending on one's income. These marginal rates are sharply lower than under the old tax laws. Thus, while tax-exempt municipal bonds are still free of federal tax, the advantage they have over taxable bonds has been reduced.

Aside from current tax law, the municipal bond market must live in fear of future changes in the US tax code. Markets always extract a premium for risk, and the risk of a tax change was very high in 1985 and 1986, as the tax reform was under consideration and yields on tax-exempt municipal bonds rose relative to taxable bonds.

The tax-exempt bond market must consider other factors in addition to the tax code. Unlike the US Treasury, state and local governments do not have the ability to print money, but they can tax themselves. Municipal bonds have a credit rating that depends on assessments of the government's ability to generate sufficient tax revenues, or in some cases operational revenues, to cover its liabilities. These quality judgements can be very important. In the mid-1970s, for instance, the fiscal crisis in New York City sent that city to the brink of bankruptcy and sent the credit spreads on its outstanding bonds to extremely high levels. Default *is* possible, and the markets must examine and price that risk.

Foreign Bonds

Foreign governments and foreign corporations have from time to time tapped the US (Yankee) bond markets as a source of funds. These issues are generally denominated in US dollars, but occasionally they are denominated in the home currency of the foreign issuer. This aspect adds an additional risk, the foreign exchange risk, for dollar-based investors, and means that the bond interest rates will track the home currency yield curve, not the US Treasury curve.

Furthermore, the strength or weakness of the US dollar on foreign exchange markets will make a very big difference to whether foreigners find the US debt markets attractive as a place to raise funds. For example, in the 1980–1 period, foreigners were raising about $27 billion a year in the United States, but as the dollar kept strengthening, the debt raised declined to $17 billion annually in the 1982–3 period, and was reduced to only $2 billion in 1984. The reason for this behavior is that a strong dollar makes the debt of foreigners much more expensive to repay in terms of the home currency. Thus, the exceptional rise of the dollar, which did not end until February 1985, was a major factor in discouraging foreigners from tapping US credit markets.

When foreign bonds are issued in dollars, they trade very similarly to US corporate debt. The market makes a credit judgement, and the bonds will trade at a premium to the US Treasury yield curve based on that credit judgement. Of course, making the credit judgement is harder since one must consider country risk factors as well as company factors.

Mortgage-backed Securities

The US homeowner is an extremely active issuer of debt securities, ranking well ahead of the corporate market. Indeed, the volume (net) of funds raised annually by homeowners through mortgages is larger than the new funds raised annually by the world's largest debtor, the US government.

When a US resident buys a house (or a condominium, or a cooperative apartment), a mortgage is usually obtained from a bank or a savings and loan institution. In any case, this mortgage is often transferable – that is, it can be packaged into a marketable security and sold into the bond market. This securitizing of home mortgages is big business, as can be seen from table 13.1, and it justifies the inclusion of the homeowner as a major bond issuer, albeit through the banks, savings and loans, brokerage houses, and federal agencies that package these loans into saleable and marketable securities.

Mortgage-backed securities, however, are extremely difficult to understand. They are also on the leading edge of financial market innovations. To put these issues in their proper perspective, the next chapter is dedicated solely to the mortgage market.

14

It's All in the Packaging:
Securitization and Mortgages

The process of packaging risks so that they can be traded on Wall Street has been a major business of the 1970s and 1980s. The case of mortgaged-backed securities is one of the best examples of this phenomenon.

Mortgage-backed securities are complex debt instruments, involving a little bit of everything. They include: (1) credit risk, (2) maturity uncertainty, since homeowners have the right to prepay their mortgages before they are due, (3) government involvement through guarantees of varying quality, (4) different structures in how the individual homeowner mortgages are packaged into a security, and (5) tax uncertainty, which depends on the continued deductibility of interest for the homeowner, an item that could affect prepayments.

In this chapter we want to accomplish just two things. First, we will describe the basic ways in which mortgages are securitized. Second, we will underscore the importance of prepayment risk to the actual world of trading mortgage-backed securities.

Securitization

Three creatures of the US government – the Government National Mortgage Association (GNMA, or 'Ginny Mae'), the Federal National Mortgage Association (FNMA, or 'Fannie Mae'), and the Federal Home Loan Mortgage Corporation (FHLMC, or 'Freddie Mac') – have varying authority to take home mortgages and guarantee the timely payment of interest and principal. In some cases this is a true government guarantee, and in other cases it is dependent on the credit of the corporation created by the government. What these agencies have done constitutes the first step in the securitization of home mortgages: they have made the mortgages more standard in lending terms and credit quality.

The next step, accomplished by these agencies in conjunction with banks and brokerage houses, is to establish pools of mortgages. A pool is nothing more than a group of mortgages. Wall Street creates the pools and then sells shares in the pools.

A pool may include, for example, ten mortgages based on ten homes, sold in the same town, with mortgages running from $75,000 to $125,000 and averaging $100,000 each. This would make the original principal value of the pool $1 million. The mortgages usually would be guaranteed by one of the government-sponsored agencies (such as GNMA), packaged by the bank (or the agency), and then sold. As each homeowner pays interest and principal, the same interest and principal is passed through to the buyers of the pools. The bank or savings and loan institution that made the initial mortgage may continue to service (send the bills, pay the property taxes, etc.) the mortgage, or may sell the servicing rights. In any case, the buyer of the pool is paid the interest and principal from the mortgages in the pool, and these are known as pass-through securities.

A problem with pass-through securities is that the combination of principal and interest received by the buyer every month may vary. As homeowners in the mortgage pool move, buy new houses, pay off the old mortgages, and take on new ones, the interest and principal payments of the pool will change. As will be discussed in detail later, this can affect the value of the security, and it directly affects its expected average life.

Indeed, while most mortgages are made for 30-year maturities, the average life of a pool of mortgages in normal times is thought to be around 12 years. Of course, this will vary depending on changes in the general level of interest rates and for different regions of the United States. This latter point can depend on things like divorce rates, which are higher in California (meaning that houses get sold and mortgages paid down) than in Vermont (where couples stay together longer and keep their houses, and mortgages, longer).

Collateralized Mortgage Obligations

The problem of uncertain maturity led to an innovation known as the CMO or *collateralized mortgage obligation*. CMOs are securities that represent a claim on pools of mortgages, and in this sense they are similar to pass-through securities. They differ dramatically, however, in how interest and principal are allocated over time.

In a pass-through pool of $5 million, if one homeowner repays his mortgage in the fourteenth month, and that mortgage was for $150,000, then that $150,000 will be distributed on a percentage share basis to all the owners of the pool at the time the prepayment is made. This is the essence of the pass-through format.

In a CMO this prepayment will be handled differently. The CMO is divided into three or four 'tranches,' or pools within the overall pool. Any prepayments that are made go first to pay off investors in tranche 1. Later, as more prepayments are made, investors in tranche 1 will be fully repaid and they will receive no more interest or principal. At that point, the next prepayments go to reduce the outstanding principal of tranche 2, and so on. The last tranche, the Zth tranche, will be the last to mature and to be fully repaid.

Investors have a choice. They can buy tranche 1 and expect early repayment, probably in only a few years, or they can buy tranche Z, the last one, and expect that this mortgage-backed obligation will mature in 15 or more years, perhaps even longer.

While CMOs are backed by mortgages just like pass-throughs, the collateral may exceed the CMO principal issue to ensure greater certainty of maturity for the earlier tranches. Other modifications have been made to the CMO structure as well. In general, these modifications are made to ensure that a portion of the investors receive interest with a certain maturity, while the investors in other tranches will bear the full burden of the maturity risk. Of course, risk has its price, so the returns on the tranches with less certain maturities will contain a premium.

Prepayments

From the preceding discussion of standard pass-throughs versus CMOs, one can see that the role of prepayments is extremely important, in that it goes the wrong way for the investor at the wrong time.

Suppose that one invests in 12 percent coupon mortgage-backed pass-through securities in a market of stable interest rates. That is, banks are still making (originating) mortgages at 12 percent for 30-year maturities. The investment is selling at par, or 100, the price at which it was originally issued. Now suppose interest rates start to fall dramatically. Mortgages become available at less than 10 percent. What happens? First, declining interest rates are good for bondholders, so initially the mortgage pool will begin to sell above par, above 100. Unfortunately, with the 12 percent coupons, the interest received each month can be reinvested only at lower rates. This, by the way, is the reinvestment risk which played a key role in duration analysis.

Then prepayments start to occur. Homeowners go to the bank and refinance their mortgages. That is, they prepay their 12 percent mortgages and take new mortgages at 9.5 percent. This saves them considerable interest over the next few years, making the refinancing worth the cost and trouble. When a homeowner refinances, there is a principal repayment made to the holders of the pass-through mortgage pool. This principal cannot be reinvested at 12 percent, but can now be reinvested only at less than 10 percent. In short, as rates fall, buyers of mortgage pass-through pools do not continue to earn 12 percent on their investment. As rates fall sharply, mortgages get prepaid, the maturity of the pool is reduced, and the repaid principal is left to be invested in new, lower-yielding assets. The prepayment is good for the homeowner, as it reduces interest expense, but it is bad for the mortgage pool investor, because it raises reinvestment risk.

CMOs allow better control over this risk because they offer choices on which tranche to buy, with varying prepayment risks. Furthermore, modifications in the CMO structure, including over-collateralization, may make some tranche maturities more certain than others.

In an environment of rising interest rates, investors would welcome prepayments. The prepaid principal could be reinvested at higher interest rates. Of course, with interest rates rising, the number of prepayments falls. The incentive to prepay is not there.

An example of how much prepayments can effect the value of mortgage-backed securities occurred early in 1986. From the fall of 1985 to the spring of 1986, interest rates dropped dramatically. In this short period, the yield on US Treasury securities of 20-year maturities fell from 10.5 percent to below 8.0 percent. As interest rates fell, mortgage rates dropped as well, and homeowners started to prepay and refinance in droves. This increased the reinvestment risk for mortgage-backed securities tremendously, especially for the high-coupon pools compared with the low-coupon pools. Not surprisingly, the prices of these pools diverged sharply, depending on their coupons. Mortgage-backed securities based on high-coupon pools either lost value or barely held their value, depending on the actual prepayment experience of the individual pool. On the other hand, securities backed by low-coupon mortgages saw their prices rise, although not by nearly as much as the rally in the US Treasury bond market.

Conclusion

Many of the forces that have been sweeping Wall Street are embodied in the phenomenon of mortgage-backed securities. Standard homeowner mortgages have been packaged into securities and sold by the billions. These securities include varying qualities of credit risk. They also have uncertain maturities and uncertain durations. This uncertainty reflects the prepayment options available to homeowners should interest rates fall. Thus, these securities involve the securitization process, the use of options, complex duration calculations, and so on.

Wall Street has excelled at creating a variety of packages, with different risk characteristics, to suit various investor tastes for risks, by type and quantity. As much as any development, the mortgage-backed market exemplifies the ability of Wall Street to innovate and meet the needs of various institutions and individuals to better manage risk during volatile times.

15

Passing the Risky Buck:
Financial Futures and Options

The sharp increase in the volatility of interest rates in the 1970s and the early 1980s as compared with the staid and quiet 1950s and 1960s created a new concern for investors and financial executives: interest rate risk. Since the beginning of the floating exchange rate regime, multinational companies and multi-currency investors attempted to manage the risk of foreign currency fluctuations by hedging in forward currency markets. In an analogous development, attention is now paid to managing exposure to interest rate fluctuations.

In response to the unprecedented volatility in dollar interest rates, new financial markets developed to reduce substantially the costs of shifting among parties the risk associated with interest rate changes. Interest rate futures and interest rate options have become well established financial instruments in a complex and rapidly evolving market.

There is a number of misconceptions about the hedging assurance actually provided by interest rate futures. But when properly used, financial futures (and options) can help some companies to maintain their operating and financing flexibility by insulating them from the adverse effects of interest rate risk, however, the use of financial futures and options must be part of a carefully thought out, corporate-wide financing strategy.

The first step in dealing with 'interest rate risk' is to place it in its proper economic and corporate perspectives. Specifically, we want to work toward (1) a definition of interest rate risk, and (2) a general risk management framework, both to assess the company's exposure to such risk and to determine whether this risk should be

A version of this article was originally published by the Chase Manhattan Bank in the 'Chase Financial Quarterly.'

managed at all. The purpose of the introductory section is to establish that, for most non-financial corporations, the management of interest rate risk should be a 'residual' stragegy. That is, it should be integrated with, and subordinated to, management's longer-run financial planning.

After considering the broader questions of what interest rate risk is, and whether is should be actively managed, we then turn to an investigation of financial futures and options, evaluating their usefulness as tools for hedging corporate exposure to such risk.

Interest Rate Risk and Corporate Finance

Interest rate risk is most commonly thought of as the potential for losses caused by changes in interest rates when funding long-term investment with shorter-term borrowings, or vice versa. As many financial institutions have learned through experience, unanticipated movements in interest rates can result in large portfolio losses (and gains) when a portfolio of assets and liabilities is 'mismatched' across maturities. The savings and loan industry, traditionally using short-term borrowings to finance long-term mortgages, offers a classic (if extreme) illustration of interest rate risk. When interest rates rose unexpectedly, financing costs rose while asset values declined, squeezing cash flow and severely decreasing net worth.

It is important to recognize, however, that the gains and losses from movements in interest rates represent only the 'arithmetic' of interest rate risk. That is, the heightened variability of interest rates is really only a symptom of more fundamental developments in the economy. The corporate treasurer can devise *ad hoc* short-run strategies that attempt to deal directly with the symptoms, while ignoring the causes. But a more enlightened approach to the problem – one that can be incorporated into a systematic, long-range financial planning process – would be grounded in an understanding of the underlying determinants of 'interest rate risk.'

It is an economic commonplace that changes in interest rates are strongly correlated, at least over long periods of time, with changes in inflation. If, for example, everyone knew with certainty that inflation would be 10 percent per year forever, then all interest rates would incorporate a 10 percent inflation 'premium' in addition to a relatively constant real rate of interest. Investors would demand the premium because the principal would be repaid at a later date in money depreciated by inflated prices. Borrowers would pay the premium because they would benefit from using the funds now and repaying later in cheaper dollars.

In the real world, of course, inflation expectations are not held with certainty, and substantial forecasting errors are the norm. But in the long run, say decade by decade, and predicted relationship between interest and inflation rates provides a good working approximation of economic realtiy. As shown by figure 15.1, interest and inflation rates in the 1950s were both at relatively low levels, and they rose in tandem in the 1960s and 1970s. There were, to be sure, some unpredictable lags in the adjustment of interest rates to inflation in the process of moving from the low-inflation 1950s to the high-inflation 1970s. The general relationship, however, is clearly borne out by our own experience. And the experience of the United States is not uncommon. High-inflation countries are uniformly high-interest-rate countries. This means that, over the long run, the risk associated with sustained high interest rates is nothing more than the risk of sustained high inflation.

Before considering 'interest rate risk,' then, management should attempt to assess its exposure to 'inflation risk.' Because the problems of interest rate risk and inflation risk are interwined, they will have to be managed together. But the appropriate first step in dealing with interest rate risk is to determine the long-run exposure

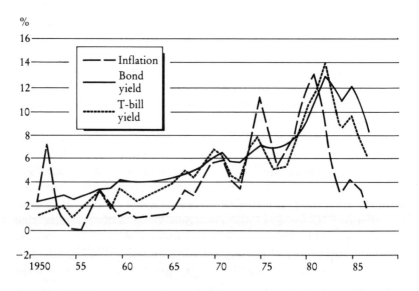

Figure 15.1   US interest rates track inflation over the long run, 1950–86.

of the firm to changes in the rate of inflation. This assessment should allow management to choose a long-term debt structure which offsets that risk.

The choice between fixed-rate and floating-rate debt should be a conscious strategic decision reflecting management's approach to inflation risk. Floating-rate debt means, of course, higher interest payments during periods rising inflation. And, for those companies whose real earnings are hurt by increases in inflation, long-term fixed-rate, debt provides a better hedge against inflation risk, matching lower real interest costs with lower real profits in an inflationary environment. But, for companies whose long-run operating profitability keeps pace with inflation, higher inflation will also mean higher revenues to offset this increase in financing costs. For such companies, fixed-rate debt effectively increases the exposure to inflation risk, providing a windfall gain to the corporate borrower when earnings increase with rising inflation, and an unexpected loss when the rate of inflation and revenue growth slows.

Thus, while fixed-rate debt may appear to eliminate interest rate risk by fixing interest payments, it actually represents a bet on inflation – an exposure to inflation risk. Floating-rate debt, by contrast, offers a long-run hedge against inflation risk, even though nominal interest payments will fluctuate. The real or inflation-adjusted interest rate on floating-rate debt is really fixed, while the real interest rate of fixed-rate debt floats. And, for long-range financial planning, the relative certainty about the company's *real* interest costs provided by the use of floating-rate debt may override all other considerations.

In the short run, however, the relation of interest rates to observed rates of inflation is extremely variable and thus unpredictable. The reasons for this are two-fold. First, the relevant relationship that between interest rates and *expected*, not actual, rates of inflation. Because the inflationary expectations built into interest rates can change abruptly, and because they often prove to be wrong, the short-run association between interest rates and inflation is much weaker than the long-run average. Second, short-run interest rates can be significantly affected by changes in monetary and fiscal policy; and these effects can register well before the inflationary inplications of the new policies are reflected in the price level. The important implication is that in the short run, which can be viewed as anywhere between, say, one day and three years, interest rate risk may not be directly related to inflation risk.

Consequently, even for those companies whose operations provide a natural hedge against inflation, floating-rate debt may not provide a sufficient hedge against interest rate risk.

Corporate Finance Perspectives

Let's begin by considering the problem from the perspective of the treasurer of a large, mature industrial company, with a demonstrated ability to maintain its average real profitability over inflationary and business cycles. Having first attempted to assess and limit the company's long-run exposure to inflation risk, the treasurer must then determine whether the remaining interest rate risk should be hedged. Once we assume that the aid of corporate management is to maximize shareholder wealth, the question reduces to whether actively managing interest rate risk will help the shareholders achieve a higher return on their investment for bearing a given level of risk.

Finance theory maintains that, in general, managing corporate risk which would otherwise increase the expected variability (as opposed to the level) of a company's earnings does not benefit shareholders. Most company-specific risks, provided they do not significantly raise the possibility of bankruptcy, can be managed more efficiently by the shareholders through portfolio diversification. By pooling many different inividual risks, the shareholder is protected against a major calamity affecting a particular company or industry.

To the extent that interest rate volatility represents a systematic, economy-wide phenomenon which cannot be eliminated by investors' diversification, there may be some value to shareholders in management's reducing exposure to short-run deviations from the interest rate-inflation parity. In the main, however, the management of interest rate risk (for non-financial corporations) should *not* be designed simply to 'smooth' small fluctuations in earnings. Nor should it attempt to hedge the exposure of *financial* assets only, without placing such exposure within the context of the total, corporate-wide, sensitivity to interest rate changes.

Its principal aim should instead be to offset the risk that wide swings in rates will endanger the financing and operating flexibility of the company. If the risk is so large that a wrong 'bet' on interest rates leads to bankruptcy, or to a major alteration of the business plan, then it makes sense to establish an active hedging program to minimize that risk. If the company's interest rate risk is not of this order, then a more passive strategy, involving perhaps a periodic monitoring of the overall corporate exposure, is probably sufficient.

Assessing Interest Rate Risk

To illustrate this point, consider the case of a well capitalized, multinational company borrowing short-term funds in many of the world's money markets. Such a firm is likely to have a revenue/cost performance record which tracks inflation fairly well over, say, a five-year cycle. Although inflation and interest rate risks are not managed directly, the long-term risk that abrupt changes in inflation or interest rates will lead to financial distress is very small. At any given time, the company will be taking many small, partly offsetting, bets on inflation and interest rates (and on exchange rates as well), which, when aggregated over time and viewed in relation to the capitalization of the company, result in a low-risk profile. A large firm can weather a good number of individually adverse outcomes without unduly harming its operations. To extend the gambling analogy, the player placing a larger number of bets (of roughly the same size) expects to lose a few, but these are likely to be offset by other bets.

Consider also, however, a smaller growth company with narrowly concentrated operations, and with a more uncertain relationship between real profitability and inflation. Because individual financing decisions can have a major impact on the overall company, management does not get the benefit of taking many potentially offsetting bets. In this case, a sharp swing in interest rates could do severe damage to the company's operating cash flow, imparing its ability to raise capital and carry out its business plan. Such a company may have a very large exposure to interest rate risk – an exposure that should probably be managed directly.

Having established the need to reduce this exposure, the corporate strategist will then want to consider the use of financial futures and options. The next several sections provide an introduction to these new financial instruments, dispel some common misconceptions, and evaluate their relative merits as tools for managing interest rate risk.

Financial Futures

Basic Concepts

Like commodities futures, financial futures contracts are agree-
ments by which two parties set a price today for a transaction that
will not be completed until a specified date in the future. For
example, consider a futures contract for $1 million on 90-day
Treasury bills, deliverable in six months, and priced at 88.00 (based
on 100.00 being par), for an annualized discount of 12.00 percent.
These terms oblige the seller of the futures contract to deliver a $1
million 90-day Treasury bill to the buyer on the specified date, six
months in the future, for the price set today, 88.00

At the end of the six months, the prevailing discount on 90-day
Treasury bills is not likely to be exactly 12.00 percent, and one party
will make a profit – and the other party a loss – equal to the difference
between the actual (spot) price and the price set six months
previously. The buyer of the futures contract will profit if interest
rates decline below the rate set by the contract (or, equivalently, if
prices rise above the price set by the contract), while the seller
stands to gain if interest rates rise and prices fall below the value set
by the contract. As illustrated in figure 15.2, the gains and losses are
'symmetric,' which is to say that the buyer's gains are the seller's
losses, and vice versa. (In fact, these gains or losses are paid along
the way, and not at the end of the contract. This is the 'mark-
to-market' feature of the futures instrument, which will be
discussed later.)

One possible corporate use of financial futures is to convert a
floating-rate loan into a synthetic fixed-rate loan. For example, the
borrower of a 90-day floating-rate Eurodollar loan could use the
Eurodollar futures market to 'lock in' his interest rate for the next
rollover date. That is, assuming a $1 million loan is scheduled for
repricing in June, the borrower could sell in March a $1 million
90-day Eurodollar CDs futures contract, promising to take delivery
in June. If interest rates rise, the higher interest payments will be
offset by an equal gain on the futures contract. If interest rates
decline, however, the benefit of lower interest payments for the
June quarter will be offset by an equal loss on the futures contract
(as the price of the contract will have increased). By using interest
rate futures to 'fix' a floating-rate loan, the borrower in effect
eliminates the risk of higher interest payments; but he also gives up
the chance to gain from an interest rate decline (figure 15.2 provides
an example).

Assume:
(1) Spot 90-day Eurodollar rate = 12.00 percent (discount basis)
(2) Three-Month future contract Eurodollar rate = 12.00 percent (price = 88.00, discount basis)
Because the futures market offers opportunities to change the interest rate associated only with future repricings of the Eurodollar loan, the borrower is stuck with the 12.00 percent interest rate for the next three months.

The borrower of the $1 million floating-rate Eurodollar loan can take his chances on where rates will be in three months (the rollover date), or be can lock in the 12.00 percent offered by the futures market by selling a three-month $1 million Eurodollar futures contract. (As we will discuss later, the futures market rate can either be below, equal to, or above the current rate, depending on the shape of the yield curve.)

If rates go to 14.00 percent in three months, interest payments on the $1 million loan for the next quarter will rise by $5000. This increase, however, will be offset exactly by a $5000 profit on the Eurodollar futures contract.

Alternatively, if rates go to 10.00 percent in three months, the next quarter's interest payments on the $1 million loan would fall by $5000, but the seller of the futures contract would lose $5000 on the price increase.

Finally, if interest rates had remained constant at 12.00 percent, and the borrower had not used the futures market, his interest expense for the next quarter would be the same as that of the previous quarter.

Figure 15.2   Financial futures

This is the essence of the financial futures market: trading interest rate risks. A hedge exists only when one party has a risk somewhere in his portfolio that he can offset with a futures market contract, but this means trading away the opportunity for gain as well as the potential for loss.

The Yield Curve

The relationship between current interest rates and the rates built into the corresponding futures contracts depends on the shape of the yield curve. Recall that the shape of the yield curve reflects the rates of interest paid on progressively longer maturities of the same financial instrument. The yield curve thus embodies investors' expectations about the future direction of interest rates. A sharply upward-sloping yield curve, in which yield on longer maturities are considerably higher than those on shorter maturities, reflects the market concensus that rates are more likely to rise in the future. An 'inverted' yield curve, by contrast, means that rates are expected to fall.

Thus, whether the futures market offers an interest rate for a future period that is less than, equal to, or greater than today's rate on the same financial instrument is determined largely by those expectations embodied in the yield curve. The following example should help explain why.

Investors are always offered a choice, say, between (1) buying a 90-day Treasury bill today, and rolling it over into another 90-day Treasury bill in three months; or (2) buying a 180-day Treasury bill today. If the investor takes the first option (rolling over successive 90-day bills), then his total six-month return is uncertain. But, if he also locks in a return on the 90-day Treasury bill he plans to buy in three months (by buying a Treasury bill futures contract), then his six month return on the transaction becomes certain. This means that he can compare the return on the rollover option in combination with the futures position to the return on simply buying a six month Treasury bill.

Because both returns are certain, investors facing the choice will always choose the option offering the higher return. This process (known as 'arbitrage') of comparing returns and electing the alternative promising the higher return guarantees that the futures market rates will reflect the expectations embodied in the yield curve of the underlying financial instrument. In this example, the arbitrage process ensures that, if 6-month Treasury bills are yielding considerably less than 3-month Treasury bills, then the 90 day Treasury bill futures rate (net of tax and liquidity considerations) will be below the current (spot) 90 day Treasury bill rate.

Because the futures markets are constantly arbitraged against the existing 'cash' markets by the major financial institutions around the world, the rates and prices offered in the futures market bear a strong resemblance to the rates in the financial, or cash, markets. If they did not, then these institutions would be forgoing riskless profit opportunities – a situation which is not likely to last for any appreciable length of time. The result, as suggested, is that the futures prices (and hence interest rates) for the different contract maturities of short-term instruments like Treasury bills and Eurodollars will closely reflect the shape of the yield curve on those instruments.

For example, if the yield curve for Eurodollar rates is inverted, the futures market will reflect this inversion by setting the interest rate on the contract deliverable in three months higher (by setting the price lower) than the rates on the contracts due in six or nine months. This means that futures do not allow the investor or the borrower to lock in today's interest rate. As the above example illustrates, one can lock in only the rate offered by the market, which will necessarily reflect the shape of the yield curve.

The futures market thus offers insurance to borrowers only against *unexpected* changes in interest rates. When the yield curve is sharply upward-sloping, and interest rates are thus expected to rise, the financial manager will be able to lock in only the higher interest rate expected by the futures market. Hence, the borrower will be protected only against increases in interest rates above those already impounded into the current yield curve.

It is also important to remember that the shape of the yield curve can change, even when spot interest rates do not. That is, because the market may change its expectations about future interest rates during the period covered by a given futures contract, rolling over a series of short-term futures contracts to hedge a longer-term commitment does not provide the equivalent of a fixed-rate commitment. When the rollover date arrives, the company will be able to lock in only the then current futures market rate, not the rates that prevailed at the time of the original hedge. Thus, rolling over futures contracts to hedge a floating-rate loan will not protect the borrower (beyond the period covered by the contract already in effect) from a sudden upward shift in interest rate expectations that takes place while the contract is in effect. Furthermore, because the futures markets offer contracts with at most two-year maturities, this 'rollover risk' means that futures cannot be used to hedge for the longer-term planning horizon.

The futures–yield curve relationship also means that use of the futures market cannot provide the borrower with cheaper financing costs, or the lender with a higher expected return, than what is currently available in the financial markets. When a borrower uses futures to convert a 3-month floating-rate loan into a 1-year fixed-rate obligation, the synthetic fixed rate of interest paid will not end up differing greatly from the rate on 1-year debt instruments. Not surprisingly, there is no free lunch in the futures market.

The Margin Account

To purchase a futures contract, the buyer does not pay cash for the full or partial value of the underlying investment. Only a small cash outlay, called the 'margin requirement,' is necessary. The investor is obliged to maintain a minimum amount in a margin 'account' throughout the life of the contract, as a kind of good faith assurance that all future commitments under the terms of the contract will be met. Any amounts over this level may be withdrawn and invested.

But, if a fall in the price of the futures position causes the value of the account to fall below the minimum level, additional cash must be deposited. Brokerage firms often pay interest (this is negotiable) on margin accounts, so that these are not, strictly speaking, idle funds.

Cash Flows and the Mark-to-market Feature

A feature of futures markets that can make otherwise perfect hedges substantially less than perfect in the eyes of corporate treasurers is the 'mark-to-market' requirement. The value of an interest rate futures contract reflects, of course, the expected yield on the underlying financial instrument when the contract expires. As expectations shift, spot interest rates change, the shape of the entire yield curve may change, and thus the value of futures contracts changes. This happens continuously. At the close of each day's trading, futures exchanges mark all accounts to their current market value, debiting the losers' and crediting the winners' margin accounts in cash.

As can be imagined, the balance in the margin account may fluctuate widely during the term of the contract. So, even while use of the futures market can lock in a particular interest rate over a period of time, the daily mark-to-market feature makes the actual timing of the holder's cash inflows and outflows highly unpredictable over that same period.

For instance, consider the strategy of using Treasury bill contracts to transform a floating-rate loan of $10 million into a 1-year fixed rate loan. The procedure would be to sell ten 3-month futures, ten 6-month features, and ten 9-month futures contracts. The interest rate on the initial three-month period would be determined by the prevailing spot rate, but each successive three-month period can be locked in by buying this 'strip' of futures contracts. Over time, the futures positions will be 'unwound' and the gains (losses) on futures will offset the higher (lower) interest rate payments for the three-month period in question. At least, that is what happens in principle.

More likely, the actual cash flows, while offsetting on a cumulative basis by the *end* of the year, will follow an unpredictable pattern *during* that year. Suppose after two months the entire yield curve shifts upward by 100 basis points. Then all of the futures contracts will increase in value by $2500 each; or, on the 30 contracts, by $75,000. This is cash credited to the hedger's account, which, if interest rates do not shift again, will compensate for the higher interest payments to be made over the next ten months.

But if interest rates decline across the yield curve by 100 basis points after the first two months, the company would suffer a *loss of* $75,000 on the 30 futures positions. While this loss will eventually be offset by lower interest payments over the next ten months, the uncertain pattern of cash flows makes even short-term cash management somewhat problematic.

Unfortunately, in hedging with financial futures, it is not only the timing of cash flows that is uncertain, but often the cumulative outcome as well. The examples offered up to this point may have given the impression that financial futures will completely insulate the user against specific interest rate risks. In moving from the basic theoretical concepts to the practical management of interest rate risk, however, I want to impress on the reader that most actual hedging situations will not match the textbook cases presented so far, or, now for the bad news.

Futures Provide Rather Less than Perfect Hedges

Basis Risk

Assuming that management has first correctly assessed its real economic exposure to changes in interest rates, there still remains another serious pitfall in hedging with financial futures. The spread between the interest rates on the instrument being hedged and on the instrument doing the hedging (futures contract) may not be stable. This interest rate spread is called the 'basis,' and uncertainty about this spread is known as *basis risk.*

If, for instance, a borrower wants to convert a prime-based bank loan into a synthetic fixed-rate loan using 90-day Treasury bill futures, then any *changes* in the spread between the Treasury bill rate and the prime rate will make the conversion less than perfect. If the prime and Treasury bill rates do not move in lock-step, the relationship between Treasury bill rates and prime will shift. This means that the hedger may still suffer economic losses (or enjoy unexpected gains) arising from interest rate fluctuations. For certain combinations of financial instruments, this risk of a change in the basis can be substantial.

The only short-term futures market instrument offering substantial liquidity as far forward as 18 months is the 90-day Treasury bill

contract. Mainly for this reason, Treasury bill futures are commonly used to hedge floating-rate bank loans tied to prime. In view
of the historical relationship between prime and three-month
Treasury bill rates, basis risk should be cause for some concern.

To help illustrate the magnitude of the basis risk problem, figure
15.3 presents the quarterly average interest rates for both 90-day
Treasury bills and bank prime rates from 1977 through 1986. Figure
15.4 shows the spread between the quarterly average rates, thus
providing a longer-run view of the basis risk involved. From these
charts, it is clear that, although the rates do move in a roughly
synchronous manner, the spread or basis has been highly variable
since late 1979. The general increase in the volatility of interest rates
has also made the spreads on different short-term financial
instruments considerably less stable. The effectiveness of Treasury
bills as a vehicle for hedging prime rate loans has therefore been
substantially reduced, just when the need for such a vehicle
dramatically increased.

In the actual process of setting a hedge, the transaction is completed
over a very short period – a day, or probably at most a week,
depending on the size of the hedge. This means that the hedger is
effectively locking in an interest rate spread between prime and the
Treasury bills futures rate which may not be representative of the
long-run average relationship between rates. Instead, the particular
spread locked in may be a short-term aberration. And even though
this spread does not reflect the long-run average, it nevertheless

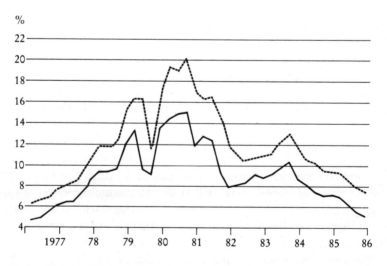

Figure 15.3   US Prime rate and 3-month Treasury bill yields, 1977–86

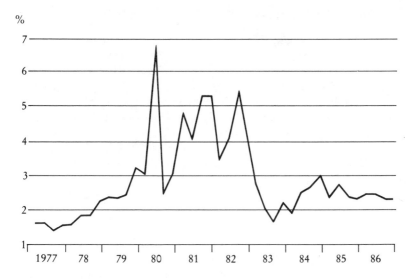

Figure 15.4   Spread between US prime rate and 3-month Treasury bill yields, 1977–86

becomes – purely by an accident of timing – the relevant basis for the borrower. Thus, the average basis risk over a quarter may not reflect the actual basis risk associated with a prime Treasury bill hedge that is transacted over the much shorter period of time.

The most sensible approach to minimizing basis risk is to use the futures instrument whose interest rate moves most closely in tandem with the debt instrument being hedged. One good example is the use of Eurodollar futures to hedge a Eurodollar loan. This significantly reduces the kind of basis risk addressed above. The Eurodollar futures market, however, is less liquid than futures contracts of US government securities.

And, even in this case, basis risk is not entirely eliminated. While one might think that interest rate changes on the underlying Eurodollar loan and the Eurodollar futures contract would be more or less the same, this is not always so. In the example that appears in table 15.1 the interest rates on bank certificates of deposit (CDs) in the cash 'spot' market are compared to rates in the CDs futures market. In November 1981, 90-day bank CDs were yielding 13 percent, while the March 1982 futures contract was at 13.14 percent – a reasonable spread. But in early January 1982, when the CD rate was again at 13 percent (a net change of zero basis points), the same March futures contract had increased by 101 basis points to 14.15

Table 15.1   Basis risk: CD futures vs. CD cash

Date	90-day CD rate, secondary market Rate (%)	Change from 11/9/81 (basis points)	Futures rate on March 1982 bank CD contract Rate (%)	Change from 11/9/81 (basis points)
11/09/81	13.00	–	13.14	–
01/05/82	13.00	0	14.15	+101
01/20/82	13.85	+85	15.05	+191

percent.* By March the rate on the futures contract would have converged with the interest rate prevailing in the cash market, because the contract specifies delivery of the cash instrument. The hedger's risk, however, would have been that the loan had to be repriced in the interim period. For example, if the repricing was scheduled for Janurary 1982, the hedger would have gained or lost (depending on the position taken) from this fluctuation in the basis. Thus, a surprising amount of basis risk exists even when using a futures contract on the same underlying instrument as the one being hedged.

The problems of basis risk are sometimes reduced by the use of more complex futures strategies involving multiple contracts across instruments and maturities. This can provide a synthetic futures instrument that fits the underlying instrument more closely than just a Treasury bill or Treasury bond contract. These strategies are worthy of case-by-case study, particularly if the basis risk problem seems severe, but are too specific for consideration here.

In summary, basis risk must be carefully assessed before hedging transactions are undertaken. Using futures as a hedging device will always entail some basis risk. In some cases, it will be substantial. Consequently, the effective use of financial futures requires some knowledge of the relationships between rates on a variety of instruments.

---

*The explanation is that the yield curve, which had been relatively flat in November, had taken on a steep positive slope by January, causing a sharp divergence between the actual and futures market interest rates. This was, of course, the result of a sharp change in short-term interest rate expectations.

Accounting vs. Economic Risk

Another pitfall for the hedger lies in the corporate accounting practice of recording assets and liabilities at historical instead of market values. Gains or losses are generally realized by accountants only when assets are sold or liabilities retired. And as a result, a company's economic exposure to interest rate variability can be quite different from its balance sheet exposure.

The stock market, as the accumulating evidence suggests, sees through accounting fictions, pricing companies according to the economic or market value of their assets and liabilities. The management of financial risks should, therefore, attempt to manage real economic, not illusory, accounting exposures.

If exposure to interest rate risk is assessed on the basis of book values, and if book values exceed market values, then management may tend to over-hedge its actual exposure. 'Over-hedging,' however, is a misnomer when using financial futures. The symmetry of futures gains and losses means that when one 'over-hedges' with futures, one has actually switched to the other side of the bet.

To see this more clearly, suppose a company purchased $10 million of bonds in the mid-1970s at par with a 9 percent coupon and, facing higher current yields, wanted to protect those bonds against a further loss of value from even higher interest rates. The company should not sell $10 million of futures contracts if the bonds have actually declined in value by $3 million. Only the current market value of $7 million should be hedged. The $3 million is gone, and the futures markets cannot retrieve lost opportunities. By hedging the face value of $10 million, management would actually be taking a *speculative* position in the opposite direction; that is, instead of merely hedging against higher interest rates, management would in effect be gambling on rates to move higher.

Futures and Options

Options Are More Flexible

Markets for buying and selling options contracts on financial instruments are now available. They are similar to financial futures in their selection of underlying financial instruments: namely, government debt contracts. They also provide a hedging alternative which minimizes or even eliminates two problems of hedging with futures: (1) the uncertainty about the timing of cash flows resulting from their mark-to-market feature; and (2) the possibility of taking a large speculative position when over-hedging.

A borrower wanting protection from rising interest rates can buy 'put' options on government debt, which will appreciate as the prices of government issues fall. The put option gives the holder the right to *sell* the underlying instrument, for a price set today, any time over the life of the contract. Figure 15.5 compares options to futures.

Investors seeking a hedge against falling rates can buy 'call' options, which will appreciate as rates fall and bond prices rise. A call option is simply the reverse of a put: it allows the holder to *buy* the underlying instrument any time up to maturity, for a price set today.

In contrast to futures, there is no mark-to-market feature with an options contract and, therefore, no fluctuating margin account to be maintained. This means that the cash flow uncertainty associated with using futures is not a problem with options.

Also unlike futures, the purchase of either a put or a call option limits the buyer's loss to the price paid for the option contract (the premium). The option buyer's potential for gain, however, is unlimited. The trading of risk is thus said to be 'asymmetrical.' The seller (writer) of options must, however, receive fair compensation for bearing the risk that others are unwilling to tolerate. Recall that unexpected interest rate swings are an economy-wide phenomenon that cannot be eliminated, only transferred (for a price) among willing market participants. In this case the seller of the financial options contract has a potential gain limited to the size of the option premium, but incurs the risk of a large, potentially unlimited loss. The fact that the seller bears more risk (relative to the futures trader) means, necessarily, that there will be a proportionately higher expected return. This means that the options premiums for insurance against adverse interest rate moves will be higher than the hedging costs associated with futures.

Nevertheless, for many companies, or for a particular situation involving a large one-time transaction, the higher cost of hedging with options may well be offset by the value of the new risk distribution, and the elimination of the cash flow uncertainty inherent in futures.

In addition, while options do not solve the basis risk problem, the 'asymmetry' of their risk distribution means that they can be used to over-insure. In the earlier example, the company purchasing a

Buyer of futures

Seller of futures

Buyer of option

Writer of option

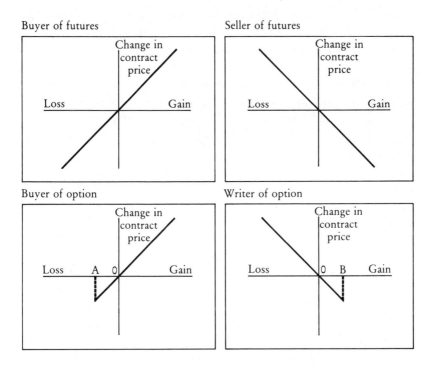

Figure 15.5   How a trader's gain or loss varies with changes in the price of a financial future or option contract. The upper right-hand quadrant shows that the buyer of a futures contract gains as the price of the contract rises, which occurs when the interest rate on the underlying asset falls. In the lower left-hand quadrant, he loses as the price of the contract falls (interest rates rise). In the upper right-hand figure, the seller of a futures contract gains as prices fall, loses as prices rise.

Movements in financial option prices are also determined by changes in interest rates on the underlying asset. The buyer of an option contract gains as the price of the option rises. This occurs for a call option when interest rates fall or for a put option when interest rates rise. As the option price falls, however, the buyer's maximum loss is limited to the premium paid, represented by OA in the lower graphs; the writer of an option contract loses as the price of the option rises, but if the option price falls his maximum gain is limited to the initial premium received, OB.

$10 million futures contract to hedge only $7 million in bonds was said to be over-hedging, but it was actually taking a speculative position in the opposite direction. In the case of options, however, hedging $10 million is still only hedging. Since the option buyer's loss is limited to the initial premium, there is no possibility of additional losses from extra contracts. Over-insuring with options simply costs a little more (i.e., is a more expensive premium for the options contracts) than a perfectly matched hedge.

Using Options to Hedge Commitments

Another distinct advantage of options is the additional flexibility they can provide in hedging commitments. To illustrate this flexibility, consider the case of a bank or insurance company which commits itself to lend money in six months at a rate set today. The lender could attempt to protect himself against an intervening change in rates by selling a six-month futures contract. The hedge may work if the transaction proceeds as planned. Suppose, however, that the borrower walks away from his commitment to borrow the money. In this case, the lender will be left holding an open futures position, exposing him to the possibility of unexpected gain or loss.

Options, however, provide protection against this uncertainty. A lender can charge a commitment fee to cover the cost of buying put option contracts to hedge the interest rate exposure. If the borrower reneges on his commitment, he loses the commitment fee. The lender, while minimizing or even eliminating potential losses, will benefit from any gains from the open position.

Although options positions can be constructed to mirror futures positions, their real value rests in their asymmetric risk characteristics. Combinations of options positions allow for a wealth of strategies, specifically tailored to the risk/reward needs of a company, or a particular situation.

In short, while futures and options both can provide insurance against interest rate risks, they will have different advantages, and thus will play somewhat different roles in hedging such risks. These roles will depend on such factors as the relevant risk/reward distribution desired by management, the ability of the operations to handle uncertain cash flows, and the amount of interest rate insurance required. Another consideration is that financial futures are older and more established, but financial options markets can be expected to mature rapidly.

Conclusion

In response to the increased volatility of interest rates, financial institutions have been forced to monitor closely and manage actively their exposure to interest rate risk. Because the sensitivity of the value of most financial assets to changes in interest rates is fairly predictable, financial futures and options should prove especially useful in managing the asset/liability exposures of savings and loan associations, commercial banks, investment banks, and insurance companies.

For most non-financial corporations, the effect of interest rate changes on the *economic* value of their assets and liabilities is more difficult to assess. Nevertheless, these companies also face risk associated with variability in inflation and interest rates; and financial managers, in many cases, should probably be reviewing this exposure in a more systematic way.

Such a review should begin by examining, and perhaps revising, the company's long-range strategic and financing policies. Because interest rates and inflation move together over long periods of time, interest rate risk is, in the long run, nothing more than inflation risk. Long-range financial planning accordingly should concentrate on the long-term exposure of the business to changes in the rate of inflation. The effects of varying inflation rates on the company's future cash flows should be simulated, if possible, at the consolidated corporate level, to gain a broad view of the company's overall *net* exposure to interest rate, inflation, and exchange rate fluctuations. (This is meant to correct the problem – often found in large organizations – of the treasury and planning offices hedging the same risk or, perhaps even more common, hedging individual risks which if left alone would cancel each other out.)

Having once established the company's long-term exposure to changes in inflation, management should attempt to minimize that exposure by choosing an appropriate long-term debt structure. For the mature, diversified company whose earnings tend to rise and fall with inflation, this may very well be a neutral strategy employing floating-rate debt as a hedge against inflation risk. Because the long-run inflation to interest rate relationship is fairly stable, the losses and gains from short-term interest rate fluctuations tend to cancel out. Consequently, a large corporation that is properly capitalized for the long haul will have the financial muscle to wait for the long-run relationship between interest rates and inflation to prevail. For such companies, attempting to hedge a modest exposure to short-run aberrations in interest rates is probably not a worthwhile exercise.

When viewed apart from the risk of inflation change, interest rate risk is thus largely a short-run phenomenon. But, for those companies with large exposures, the short run must be managed. Where there is a large possibility that unexpected changes in interest rates can cause a sharp fall in net worth, which in turn could drastically reduce the company's financing flexibility, management should give serious attention to an active hedging strategy.

Financial futures and options are the tools for hedging interest rate risk. They enable management to choose, over the short run, the interest rate exposure it wants independently of its financial structure. Their use, however, is attended by a different set of problems and considerations. Several characteristics of financial futures and options deserve special attention:

- *Financial futures can be used to trade interest rate risk. The user, in hedging, forfeits potential gains, but eliminates the chance of large potential losses caused by interest rate changes.*
- *Financial futures cannot reduce financing costs.*
- *Financial futures cannot provide a perfect hedge against unexpected interest rate movements.*
- *Interest rates on financial futures reflect the yield curve, and therefore allow the hedger to lock in only the markets' expected interest rates, not interest rates currently available in the cash market.*
- *Even though financial futures contracts can lock in an interest rate, the subsequent cash flow pattern will remain uncertain.*
- *Financial options can be used to trade risk in an asymmetric manner, allowing construction of highly complex positions.*
- *Financial options can be used to over-insure, while financial futures cannot.*
- *Financial options can be used to hedge commitments while futures cannot.*

With these considerations in mind, both financial futures and financial options can be used effectively in managing interest rate risk. Such risk management programs, though, do require constant evaluation and refinement, and these be considered as part of the costs of such insurance. Further, because the markets for trading interest risk are still evolving and the needs for managing interest rate risk are changing, today's problems and solutions may well differ substantially from those a few years hence.

Part IV
Foreign Exchange Markets

16

As the World Turns:
Currency Markets Link the Globe

Financial markets in any one country are linked to financial markets in other countries through foreign exchange markets. Flows of goods, services, and capital across national borders require the exchange of currencies, and for this reason, the foreign exchange markets truly provide the primary linkage among the world's economies.

Foreign exchange markets are some of the most efficient and fast-moving markets in today's highly integrated environment. These markets are always in operation somewhere on the globe. The day starts in Tokyo, moves to London, and then onto New York. On an average day in 1986, over $300 billion dollars would have changed hands in the various currency markets, as illustrated in figure 16.1. These flows dwarf the world's trade in goods and emphasize the role of currency markets in allocating capital around the globe.

This chapter will highlight some of the institutional aspects of currency markets. Then the focus will shift to a discussion of two concepts that demonstrate the role that currency markets play in linking the world: interest rate parity, and purchasing power parity.

Institutional Aspects

Most currency transactions involve the US dollar. That is, currency trades involve dollars for German marks or dollars for Japanese yen. If someone holds marks and wants yen, more often than not it will take two transactions, working through US dollars, to facilitate the deal. The holder of the marks will sell them for dollars, and then the dollars will be sold for yen. Only 3 percent of the world's currency transactions are direct cross-currency deals; all the rest involve US dollars.

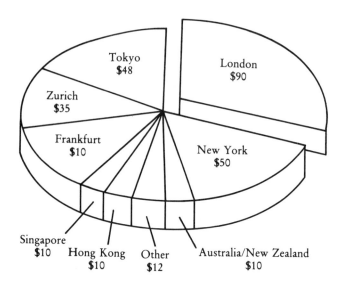

Figure 16.1   Foreign exchange market volume by trading center, 1986. The foreign exchange market is probably the world's largest financial business, with daily trading volume totalling $300 billion. Total interbank dealing in the United States has increased from a daily average of $26 billion in 1983 to over $50 billion today, with 90 percent of the nation's dealing done in New York. Trading in Tokyo has quadrupled in the last three years, owing to the deregulation of the Japanese financial markets. (*Sources:* New York Federal Reserve; Bank of England; Bank of Japan; Morgan Stanley & Co. Inc.)

On the foreign exchange markets, the key currencies are German marks, Japanese yen, British pounds, or Swiss francs versus the US dollar. In table 16.1, the percentage share of each currency versus the dollar is shown for trading in New York and London. In Tokyo, the yen is by far the dominant currency.

Trading involves four categories of participants. The commercial and investment banks serve as primary dealers, making markets in most currencies on a 24-hour basis and handling about 80 percent of all transactions. Central banks, as the keeper of the integrity of a country's money, supervise the markets and on occasion intervene as buyers or sellers in attempts to influence exchange rates. Importers, exporters, and tourists comprise the group involved in trade and tourism. Meanwhile, investors, corporate treasurers, and speculators are involved in the international transfer of capital.

Table 16.1 Daily foreign exchange turnover by currency vs. the US Dollar, 1986 (% of Total)

	London	New York
German mark	28	34
Japanese yen	14	23
British pound	30	19
Swiss franc	9	10
Canadian dollar	2	5
Other	17	9

Source: Merrill Lynch, 'Currency and Bond Market Trends,' August 18, 1986.

Most trading volume is generated by primary dealers trading among themselves, involving both hedging and speculative activity. However, the latter group – investors and corporate treasury activity – is the major non-bank source of transactions, emphasizing that capital flows are much more important than trade flows in determining daily currency transaction volume.

Somewhere between two-thirds and three-quarters of all transactions are in the spot markets. The spot currency market or cash market operates for settlement two business days after the deal is struck. The rest of the transactions involve futures, forwards, and options markets. These deals settle in the future, usually one, three, or six months ahead, on terms arranged at the time the deal is made.

The importance of these transactions with settlement well into the future can not be underestimated in terms of their impact on the process of linking domestic financial markets around the world. Because these transactions involve capital for a period of time, their costs involve the interest rates of both currencies in the deal. The relationship that describes how interest rates and the currency markets interact is called interest rate parity, and it is one of the key building blocks for understanding how international capital markets are linked.

Interest Rate Parity

The concept of interest rate parity is straightforward. International investors are seen as having two choices. For example, investors could place $1 million in 12-month Eurodollar time deposits with a major US bank in London at an interest rate of, say 6.87 percent. Or they could use the $1 million to purchase DM 2 million in the spot currency markets at a DM/$2.00 exchange rate, investing the German marks in a 12-month Euromark time deposit at an interest rate of 4.56 percent. The interest rate differential in this example is 2.31 percent, with the dollar investment yielding more than the mark investment over the same 12-month period. Investors, however, are exposed to significant foreign exchange risk, which is to say that at the end of the 12-month period, when both time deposits mature, the better investment will depend critically on whether the US dollar has appreciated or depreciated against the German mark.

This foreign exchange risk can be hedged by using the forward foreign exchange market. The investor can strike a deal today in which he agrees to deliver in 12 months's time DM2,091,200 (principal of DM2,000,000 plus DM91,200 of interest calculated at a 4.56 percent simple annual rate) in exchange for US dollars. The 12-month forward exchange rate in this example would be DM/$1.9568. This means that at the end of the period the hedged German mark investment would be converted into $1,068,700 for an increase of 6.87 percent – the same return as if the investment had been made in US dollars from the beginning. The forward exchange markets work to produce this result by adjusting the forward rate until there is no way for arbitragers to make greater returns in fully hedged investments in one currency versus another. This means that investors based in low-interest-rate countries, such as Germany or Switzerland, cannot take advantage of the higher interest rates offered by other countries without taking exchange rate risk. The cost of removing the exchange rate risk – hedging – equals the interest rate advantage. This is what is known as interest rate parity.

The equation that expresses the interest rate parity arbitrage condition is as follows:

Percentage difference		*Domestic interest*
between the spot and the		*rate minus*
forward foreign exchange	=	*foreign interest*
rate (premium or discount)		*rate.*

In this equation, the domestic interest rate and the foreign interest rate must be of the same credit risk class and of the same maturity as the forward exchange rate. Also, the assumption is made that there are no meaningful barriers to the flow of capital across countries.

Interest rate parity means that, in a country with relatively high interest rates, the forward exchange markets will trade the currency at a discount. On the other hand, low-interest-rate countries will find that their currency trades at a premium on the forward exchange markets. Indeed, the interest rate differential will equal the forward foreign exchange premium or discount.

In the example given, US interest rates exceeded German interest rates by 2.31 percent. The difference between the spot (today's) exchange rate and the forward exchange rate was also 2.31 percent. The forward rate of DM/$1.9568 indicates that the dollar would have to weaken and the mark strengthen to equilibrate investments in the two currency markets over the 12-month period.

This linkage between interest rates, spot exchange rates, and forward currency rates is extremely important. Changes in interest rates in a country will directly and immediately affect the foreign exchange markets. The spot and the forward exchange rate will have to shift to create a new premium (or discount) equal to the new interest rate differential between the two countries. Also, changes in foreign currency markets, such as when market pressures force a wider premium or discount on a currency, will result in interest rate shifts in one or both countries.

Unfortunately, interest rate parity is an arbitrage condition but not a theory of foreign exchange. One cannot tell which variable – spot exchange rates, forward exchange rates, domestic interest rates, or foreign interest rates – will adjust to a given economic shock. All four variables may shift, or only two may change.

Exchange rate determination is a topic for the next chapter. Before turning to that topic, however, it is appropriate to discuss the parallel linkage that exists between the market for goods. This is called purchasing power parity.

The Purchasing Power Parity Concept

The concept of purchasing power parity (PPP) has been articulated by many economists throughout the centuries. David Hume, writing in the 1700s in his famous essay, 'Of the Balance of Trade,' made the following statement:

And any man that travels over Europe at this day may see by the prices of commodities that money, in spite of the absurd jealousy of princes and states, has brought itself nearly to a level and that the difference between one Kingdom and another is not greater in this respect than it is often between different provinces of the same Kingdom.

Essentially, Hume was arguing that the flow of money and goods from one country to another will tend to equilibrate prices in both nations, just as the movement of merchandise from one locality to another within a given country brings prices into balance in that nation. This concept embodies an arbitrage process which pushes prices and exchange rates toward their parity values. For example if, after adjusting for exchange rates, a product is priced differently in two nations, businesses will buy it in the country where the cost is less and sell the merchandise in the nation where its value is higher, until equilibrium price levels and exchange rates (or PPP) have been reached.

As an illustration, suppose that the price of a hamburger in the United States is $1.50 and that, based on the exchange rate between the United States and the United Kingdom, it costs $1.50 to buy £1 sterling. According to PPP, hamburgers in the United Kingdom can be purchased for £1. However, if the cost of a hamburger rises to £1.50 in the UK, then in order to arbitrage this price difference, hamburgers must be bought in the United States, shipped to the UK, and sold there. However, hindrances such as taxes and import restrictions can block the arbitrage process, thus preventing the PPP principle from working perfectly. In this case, hamburger rolls may become stale on the trip over to the UK; and the UK may levy custom duties against this product. In addition, there is the time risk and costs involved in setting up the shipping, distributing, and marketing operations in the UK.

This example does not, however, invalidate the concept. Given long enough periods of time, major price differences that represent true profit-making opportunities will eventually be arbitraged to the best of the market's abilities. Further, because relative price levels and exchange rates change during the arbitrage process, PPP gives valuable insights into the direction of inflation rates and exchange rate movements, even though the purchasing power parity concept cannot be relied upon to give exact estimates of currency values.

Limitations of PPP: Causality and Overshooting

The following equation for purchasing power indicates that the percentage change in the exchange rate ($\%FX$) equals the percentage change in domestic prices ($P(D)$) minus the percentage change in the foreign price level ($P(F)$):

$$\% \triangle FX = \% \triangle P(\mathrm{D}) - \% \triangle P(F).$$

All this equation means is that exchange rates and inflation rates will come into relative balance as differentials in price levels between two different countries are arbitraged. It is important to note, however, that this equation does not indicate the direction of causality between inflation and exchange rates. Therefore, although this formula appears to provide a theory of exchange rate forecasting based on projections of inflation differentials, it should not be used as such.

One reason for this is that lags may occur between movements in the exchange rate and changes in inflation which this equation does not capture. For example, sometimes a country's currency, because of stimulative measures, may be inflating more rapidly than that of its neighbors. If this happens, the exchange rate may lag behind inflation in its response to these policies, possibly because various trade and capital restrictions exist or because the market initially fails to recognize the relative stimulus in the country. Eventually, the exchange rate depreciates, catching up with the inflation differential. On the other hand, the exchange rate may at times react more quickly than prices to policy changes and depreciate instantly, thus leading or even contributing to inflation.

A comparison of the Mexican peso devaluations of 1976 and 1982 illustrates these two possibilities. In the six years prior to the currency's first devaluation, Mexico's inflation was cumulatively 46 percent higher than that of the United States. Yet, the peso remained stable until one afternoon in September 1976, when a devaluation of the currency made up for the entire 46 percent differential. The 1982 collapse of the peso was quite different. From 1977 and 1982, Mexico's inflation was significantly higher than that of the United States. When the peso collapsed in 1982, the exchange rate did not simply adjust for the past inflation differential but overshot its purchasing power parity level – a reaction suggesting that the market believed that Mexico might devalue the currency again. In this case, the exchange rate passed parity to such a degree that in the following year inflation in the country rose dramatically, trying to catch up with the collapse in currency.

A number of factors help to decide the critical issue of whether prices will lead exchange rates or whether the reverse will occur. However, the primary determinant is monetary policy. Stimulative measures eventually will contribute to both increased inflation and a weak currency, while extremely tight policies will result in the opposite. Whether inflation or the exchange rate will take the lead is determined, in part, by the credibility of the monetary policy itself. If the market believes that restrictive measures are likely to be in place for a long time, the currency will probably move first with inflation declining later. In fact, in this situation the currency appreciation contributes to the general deflationary price path – which is what occurred in the United States in 1980. Once the Federal Reserve had shifted to stringent measures and had demonstrated that it was willing to maintain this tight policy even in a face of an economic recession, the dollar began to appreciate substantially, well before the US inflation rate declined.

Another reason why PPP cannot be used as a precise forecasting tool is that currencies can overshoot their parity levels – a very common occurrence. In this case, an exchange rate moves from an overvalued position to an undervalued status without stopping in the parity zone. There are several explanations for overshooting, two of which deserve special attention.

The first contends that, when policy changes occur, asset prices adjust faster than the prices of goods or commodities, since the former discount the future result of these measures in advance. In the short run, this means that exchange rates must over-compensate for the failure of the goods and commodity markets to respond quickly. In the long run, once prices of goods and commodities have adapted fully to the new policy environment, the exchange rate comes back into balance with purchasing power parity.

According to the second explanation, the original overvaluation is caused by a relatively tight monetary policy, and as long as this remains in place, overvaluation can persist and even become more acute. When policies finally become less restrictive, the exchange rate will weaken but will not stop in the parity zone if monetary measures remain relatively loose. The currency will stabilize in this region only if policies become more balanced during the period in which the currency is approaching its PPP level. Overshooting occurs, then, when monetary measures between two countries remain significantly different from each other, with the underlying forces continuing to push the exchange rate away from purchasing power parity.

Calculating PPP Values

In order to determine whether a currency is overvalued or undervalued, the PPP exchange rate must first be calculated. To do this, a base year is chosen during which the inflation and exchange rates are assumed to have been in 'equilibrium.' In this case, 1973 will be used. At that time, the wholesale price index was 50.11 for the United States (1980 = 100, IMF data) and 69.37 for Germany. The mark/dollar exchange rate averaged 2.6726 during the year. For 1985, the price index equaled 114.9 for the United States and 121.9 for Germany. Based on the formula shown previously, the PPP exchange rate is equal to DM/$2.05, the rate that would have existed if purchasing power parity had held perfectly between the German mark and the dollar over the 1973–5 time span.* When this rate is compared with an average mark/dollar exchange rate for 1985 of 2.94, the US currency appears to have been seriously overvalued in 1985 – by 43 percent.

The choice of the base period can be critical. It should be lengthy enough so that the long-term relationship between the exchange rates and prices can be captured, but not so protracted that structural changes in the economy and the markets distort the analysis. In table 16.2 PPP calculations are presented using three different base years and a regression projection. Only when the 1960s are employed does the parity exchange rate sharply differ from the others computed. The 1970s are considered more appropriate to use as a base for these calculations because they

Table 16.2   Purchasing power parity projections for 1986(3)[a]

	German mark per dollar	Yen per dollar
1986(3) actual	2.06	156.0
1968(1) base	2.65	237.0
1973(1) base	2.05	205.0
1976(1) base	1.97	207.0
Regression forecast[b]	2.09	175.0

[a] All calculations use wholesale price indices.
[b] Functional form of the regression is

$$\log (FX) = a + b\log \left(\frac{WPI\ foreign}{WPI\ US} \right)$$

where expected coefficients are a = 0 and b = 1.

*The computation could also have been accomplished using the following method. Here, ratios of German to US price indices are calculated for both 1973 and 1985 (i.e., 69.37/50.11 = 1.3844 and 121.9/114.9 =1.0609, respectively). Then, the ratio of the 1985 to the 1973 price calculation (1.0609/1.3844 = 0.7663) is multiplied by the 1973 (base) mark/dollar rate (0.7663 × 2.6726 = 2.05), resulting in DM/$2.05.

better reflect the realities of the floating exchange rate period. Based on these calculations, the partity zone for the mark-dollar rate probably lay between DM/$1.97 and DM/$2.09, meaning that the mid-September 1986 exchange rate of DM/$2.05 was close to the PPP value. For the Japanese currency, the parity zone ran from yen/$175 to yen/$207. However, the mid-September exchange rate of 155 was below this range, indicating that the yen had moved from undervalued status a year ago to an overvalued position, as illustrated in figures 16.2 and 16.3.

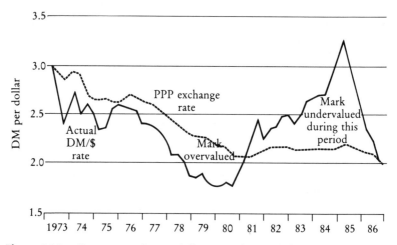

Figure 16.2   German marks per dollar: actual vs. purchasing power parity, 1973(1) base

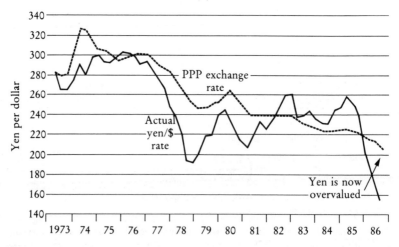

Figure 16.3   Japanese yen per dollar: actual vs. purchasing power parity, 1973(1) base

The Limits of Arbitrage Relationships

Interest rate parity and purchasing power parity are both arbitrage relationships. That is, they describe price relationships between comparable assets or goods in two countries that must hold unless investors are forgoing opportunities to make a riskless profit. This is not something the investor community is likely to do for long. And if either interest rate parity or purchasing parity fails to hold, then the likely reason is the existence of certain market barriers, such as tariffs or capital controls, that make riskless arbitrage impossible.

Arbitrage relationships describe only the relationship among a set of variables – in this case currencies, goods prices, and interest rates. They do not explain which variable will move when; arbitrage relationships assert only that one, some, or all of the variables will adjust to each other in the prescribed manner. This means that, by themselves, arbitrage concepts cannot be used for forecasting exchange rates, interest rates, or inflation rates.

What these concepts do provide is an explicit linkage between the goods and asset markets in one country and the goods and asset markets in another country. The linkage is the spot and forward foreign exchange market. Understanding these linkages and the key arbitrage relationships is the first step in describing why exchange rates move. The next step involves developing a theoretical approach that is consistent with these arbitrage concepts, and that also attempts to establish the source and the direction of causality – that is, what drives exchange rates.

17

As the World Turns, the Sequel:
the Determination of Exchange Rates

More than any other markets, foreign exchange markets link the world and testify to the growing integration and globalization of the world's financial arena. Multinational corporations, selling goods around the world, must constantly deal in foreign exchange markets to acquire the currencies they need to conduct their daily business. Investors with multi-currency portfolios also use foreign exchange markets to shift capital from one national market to another.

In the previous chapter, certain conceptual linkages, known as interest rate parity and purchasing power parity, were discussed. These theories, which describe arbitrage relationships between interest rates, inflation, and exchange rates, emphasize the role that exchange rates play in linking domestic markets to each other. They provide a few extremely valuable insights into the question of how exchange rates are determined. They do not, however, provide a complete framework in which to analyze currency values.

Economists tend to disagree more often than agree on the applicability of various theories of exchange rate determination. The analysis presented here takes a strong stand that currency values can and should be analyzed in a manner that emphasizes the role played by exchange rates in international asset allocation. The approach, however, is controversial.

Currencies, Risk, and Return

From our perspective on Wall Street, currencies are no different than any other asset. Value is determined by a comparison of the risks and returns available on competing assets. In the world of currencies, one is essentially investing in the performance of a country, and the appropriate comparisons concern the expected returns offered by a country and its risk relative to other countries.

Countries can offer returns in two general ways. They can provide high interest rates relative to inflation prospects, which reward fixed-income investors with relatively high real returns; or they can offer a healthy, dynamic economy, from which equity investors can profit as share prices rise.

For the most part, these two methods of offering returns do not occur together. High real interest rates, as noted in chapter 10 on yield curves, are most often associated with a very restrictive monetary policy. Such a monetary policy generally is imposed to reduce an inflation rate that is too high or to stop a rapid currency depreciation. The result of a tight monetary policy, if applied for a substantial length of time, such as a year or more, is to reduce inflation and lead to currency appreciation, but at a cost of reduced economic growth and, perhaps, even a recession.

On the other hand, it is possible, and some would say preferable, for strong economic growth to be fostered by an even-handed monetary policy. That is to say, a monetary policy should not be too expansionary, creating a short-lived boom, only to be followed by rising inflation and the need to run a restrictive monetary policy. Rather, monetary policy should be run in a stable fashion, producing positive real interest rates consistent with the country's long-run growth potential.

A prime example of tight monetary policy leading to currency strength was the Federal Reserve's commitment in the 1980–2 period to reduce inflation, at all costs. Real interest rates rose to historical highs and the dollar rebounded from its days of currency depreciation in the 1977–9 period. This tight monetary policy, however, led to a world recession. The strength of the dollar resulted purely from the restrictive monetary policy and high real interest rates, not from a healthy economy.

In 1982, monetary policy was eased and a major tax cut was enacted. The effects of a less restrictive monetary policy and a massively expansionary fiscal policy led to very strong economic growth in the United States in 1983 and 1984. This dynamic growth, at a time when much of the rest of the world was growing only sluggishly, provided strong incentives for world investors to send capital to the United States to take advantage of booming equity markets and a strong economy. As a result, the US dollar continued to appreciate during this period (figure 17.1).

On the return side of the ledger, then, prospects for currency appreciation depend either on a tight monetary policy and high real interest rates, or on a healthy, growing economic environment. Both conditions will attract international investors and lead to currency strength – if the risks are not too great.

Relative risk assessment is just as critical as evaluating prospective relative returns. Risks that can affect either monetary policy or real economic growth – the two sources of returns – are the key ones to investigate. We will cover a few of the more important ones here.

Inflation Risk

Inflation is a measure of the speed with which a given currency is losing its purchasing power or being depreciated in terms of the quantity of goods and services it can buy. Over the long run, a country that runs an inflation rate relatively higher than its trading partners is very likely to see its currency decline in value relative to the other currencies. This relationship, known as purchasing power parity (PPP), was discussed in the previous chapter.

Exchange rate determination, however, is a forward-looking process. In the case of high inflation and a weak currency, the markets are essentially asking if the causes of the inflation excess of

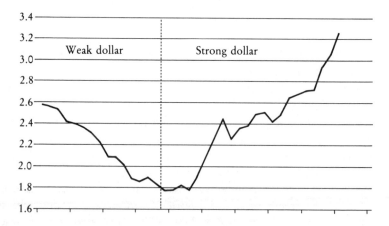

Figure 17.1   The fall and rise of the dollar: DM per dollar, 1976–1985. The end of the weak dollar period is dated at October 6, 1979, when the Federal Reserve Chairman Paul Volcker announced a shift in Fed policy to strict M1 targets.

the past are likely to continue or to be reversed. The answer is usually found by investigating the monetary policy stance of the country. As noted above, if a country shifts to a very tight monetary policy with high real interest rates, it is providing attractive relative returns for international investors, and currency appreciation is likely to result. In addition to supporting the currency, a tight monetary policy is also aimed at reducing inflation. If market participants perceive that the monetary policy will remain tight for a reasonable length of time, perhaps a year or more, then the currency markets will expect the policy to reduce inflation over a period of years. Consequently, the currency will gain value relative to other currencies immediately, despite the fact that the progress toward reducing inflation may take a long time. Expectations are the key. Just as policies expected to reduce inflation produce a strong currency, any set of policies that risks higher inflation, regardless of the time frame in which the inflation may occur, are usually detrimental to a currency's value (figure 17.2).

Trade and External Balance

The difference between a country's goods and service exports (+) and its imports (−) determines its external balance. A country with

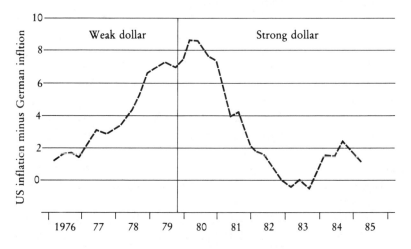

Figure 17.2   US–German inflation differential, 1976–85.
During this period, inflation differentials widened against the United States in the weak-dollar period, and inflation differentials narrowed in favor of the United States in the strong-dollar period. This inflation behavior is broadly consistent with purchasing power parity.

a deficit must finance it by attracting capital from foreign sources, while a country with a surplus must be a net foreign investor or lender. Traditionally, relatively large trade surpluses, such as those run by Germany and Japan, are associated with currency strength, and large trade deficits, such as run by the United States in the mid-1980s, are associated with currency weakness. This traditional view, while proving correct in 1985 and 1986, was very wrong in 1983 and 1984.

Large trade deficits represent a risk of currency depreciation only when these deficits are likely to damage a country's growth potential and, therefore, make the trade deficit difficult to finance. During 1983 and 1984, the United States did have a large and growing trade deficit with the rest of the world. Many currency forecasters correctly anticipated these deficits and incorrectly projected a weak US dollar for 1983 and 1984. Instead, the US dollar reached decade-high levels against many major currencies, including the German mark and the Japanese yen.

The problem with the quick answer – that trade deficits lead to currency weakness – is that this occurs only when these deficits threaten economic growth. In 1983 and 1984 the US economy was still growing much faster than other countries' economies. During this period, the trade deficit did not noticeably impair the economy's ability to create employment opportunities, as millions of new jobs were added in these two years. Furthermore, inflation continued to decline and the economy was viewed by most observers as being healthy. As a result, capital flowed into the United States, and the trade deficit did not cause a weak dollar.

In 1985 and 1986 the situation changed. The trade deficit was beginning to affect economic growth and job creation. Employment began to decline in manufacturing, although it was still rising rapidly in service sectors. Economic growth, as measured by real GNP, slowed from the 1983–4 pace of 5 percent-plus to a sluggish rate of 2 percent for 1985–6. At the same time, the economic expansions in Europe were being consolidated at a steady, sustainable pace.

From a currency perspective, several things had happened. The trade deficit was now threatening a source of return to international investors, namely, US economic growth. And relative economic growth performance had actually shifted in favor of Europe and away from the United States. Furthermore, the risk that the trade deficit would lead to policy shifts in the United States, which would force the dollar lower was very real. Indeed, the easing of monetary policy by the United States was motivated in part to strengthen the economy through a weaker dollar and better export performance. The international meeting of the G5 countries (the United States, Japan, Germany, France, and the United Kingdom) in September 1985 confirmed this policy goal of lowering the dollar's value.

The lesson is straightforward. Where trade deficits get so large and begin to look so permanent as to threaten economic growth prospects, they will lead to currency weakness. This is not always an easy judgement to make. Rapidly growing economies almost always see their trade surpluses shrink or their deficits widen. Rapid economic growth fosters import demand. Whether or not this is healthy depends on why import demand is growing. Roughly speaking, import demand dominated by capital investment (i.e., for long-term productive purposes) is rarely a problem, while import demand fed by consumption spending can be a danger signal (figures 17.3 and 17.4).

Fiscal Policy

The relationship between fiscal policy and exchange rates is not well understood. The recent fashion in the United States has been to associate fiscal irresponsibility (i.e., the huge budget deficits of the Reagan presidency) with a strong dollar. The rationale goes as

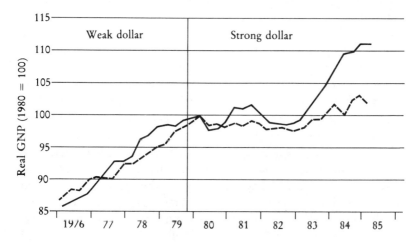

Figure 17.3   US vs. German real GNP, 1976–85.
From 1976 through 1982, real growth differentials were unimportant. The strong US expansion in 1983–84 attracted capital and strengthened the dollar, despite a widening current account deficit.

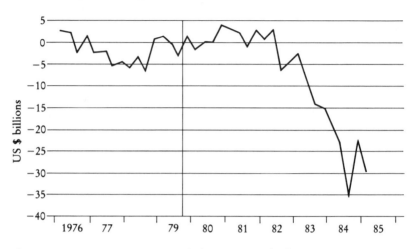

Figure 17.4   US current account balance quarterly data, 1976–85. The current account deficit did not weaken the dollar in 1983–84 owing to the very strong economc growth in the United States, which attracted international capital.

follows. High budget deficits raise interest rates and thus attract foreign capital, strengthening the currency.

This analysis is wrong, because it fails to include risk assessment. To the extent that expansionary fiscal policies lead to the risk that eventually monetary policy will be directed at financing the accumulated budget deficits with easy money and lower interest rates, large and rising budget deficits will weaken a currency. In the United States, however, the large budget deficits were accompanied by a tight to neutral monetary policy stance. That is, the well-known opposition of the Chairman of the Federal Reserve, Mr Paul Volcker, to budget deficits meant that the market did not have to worry about a dramatic easing of monetary policy to pay for the accumulated budget deficits. This was an unusual case.

In other countries where budget deficits have grown relatively large and monetary policy has not been used as a counterweight, budget deficits have led to currency weakness. For instance, in Canada the budget deficit exceeded 8 percent of GNP by certain calculations in the 1984–6 period, and the Canadian currency continued its slide against the US dollar. Other countries with budget problems in the past, such as Italy, Sweden, and the United Kingdom, provide similar examples. The hyperinflationary Latin American countries are even better illustrations. If budget deficits could result in currency strength without the help of monetary policy, these countries would certainly have strong currencies. Of course, the opposite is true.

In summary, the relationship between budget deficits and exchange rates runs through monetary policy. How is fiscal policy likely to affect monetary policy – a key source of currency returns? Loose fiscal policies can be offset by tighter monetary stances to produce currency strength. A combination of loose fiscal and loose monetary policies, however, is deadly for a currency.

Expectations and the Asset Perspective

In the approach to exchange rate determination presented here, currencies are analyzed like assets, with attention focusing on their prospective returns and risks relative to each other. This results in a tremendous emphasis being placed on market expectations about the key factors affecting a currency's returns and risks. In this regard, foreign exchange forecasting is no different from picking stocks or projecting the course of interest rates.

Exchange rate behavior can be extremely volatile. Indeed, currency movements are much more severe than changes in fundamental variables, such as inflation and trade patterns, would suggest as necessary. The reason lies with expectations. Since the collapse of the fixed exchange rate world of 1950–73, when currencies were tied to the US dollar, and the dollar to gold, there has been no anchor for exchange rates. Market participants increasingly have to make forecasts of future policy changes by different countries and then try to assess the impact of the policy shifts on currency values. These assessments, of both policy change and their effects, are constantly revised as new economic information is made available or as country leaders articulate their policy stance. It is these changing expectations that can result in volatile markets.

And volatile currency markets can be translated into volatile bond markets. Exchange rates are the mechanism that transfers economic disturbances from one country to another. This was demonstrated very clearly in the early 1980s, when the United States adopted a monetary policy based on money stock targeting that produced extremely volatile interest rates. Currency markets reflected the increased volatility, and countries around the world found themselves and their domestic interest rates profoundly influenced by this shift in US monetary policy.

The same holds true in the United States. The meetings held by the G5, during which the leaders of the United States, the United Kingdom, Germany, Japan, and France decided to weaken the dollar in September 1985, did encourage dollar depreciation. But to promote this plan, Japan forced its interest rate upward in the months following the meeting. This put temporary upward pressure on US interest rates. Later, in 1986, US desires for lower world interest rates were constrained in part, by a reluctance of the monetary authorities in Germany and Japan to lower their rates. The United States eventually went ahead on its own, but the dollar fell in value in volatile markets, as market participants saw the United States moving to a substantially easier monetary policy (and lower returns) than other countries. In turn, the US bond market reacted adversely to the decline in short-term US rates, because of fears that the policy would be inflationary and that international demand for US bonds would decline in a weak dollar environment. In essence, the consequence of lower short-term rates, weakened the dollar and partly caused higher interest rates in the US bond markets, steepening the yield curve.

The messages are important. Understanding foreign exchange markets requires a sophisticated view of how expectations affect market dynamics. And currency markets are important, even for purely domestic investors, because what happens in any market around the world can be transmitted to any other market through the currency shifts that take place.

Conclusion

18

On the Future of Wall Street

Like any other industry, Wall Street has its fashions. Today the received logic is that the financial services business is emerging from a period of revolutionary change and entering a period of prosperity and more gradual evolution. The key trends of globalization, product innovation, and securitization will continue at a more moderate pace. Market developments may not proceed so smoothly. In the case of each of these major trends, there are forces emerging that could dramatically complicate and significantly alter the future course of financial market events.

Globalization versus Trade protectionism

For instance, globalization of financial markets has depended on and followed dramatic increases in world trade. Figure 18.1 shows the extent to which growth in global trade has outstripped general world economic growth. Globalization, the process of integrating world economies, can also be seen in the dependence on imports that has occurred around the globe. For example, the relative openness of economies, as measured by the penetration of imports into domestic consumption patterns, has increased dramatically in the last decade, as shown in table 18.1.

But this trend toward freer and greater world trade is now facing the threat of rising world protectionism from almost every corner. The large trade deficit in the United States that developed in 1983 and 1984 and increased massively in 1985 and 1986 has raised the call for legislation to stop the growth of imports. The United States has raised barriers on lumber from Canada, has subsidized its own wheat production, and has limited textile imports. The list goes on and on – and it is growing. Meanwhile, Europe is afraid of an

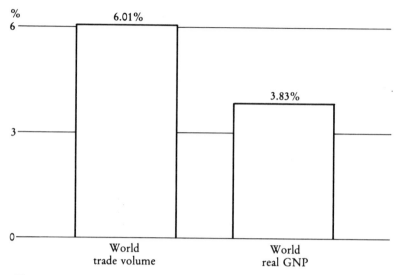

Figure 18.1   Average annual world real GNP and trade volume growth, 1960–85

invasion of Japanese products, and barriers are rising there, too. Indeed, the European Common Market has built quite a fortress around itself. And the Asian countries such as Japan, Korea, and Taiwan love to export, but they have blocked imports to a very great degree. With trade protectionism on the rise, the pace of globalization of financial markets could be threatened. Parallels with the trade wars of the 1930s should not be taken lightly.

There are factors at work, however, that promise to keep the globalization process going for several more years. First among them is the desire of governments to privatize nationalized industries. The reason that this factor spurs globalization is that the only way governments can sell large companies to the public is by establishing freer stock markets and letting foreigners in on the game: otherwise, the domestic equity markets as currently regulated (and stifled) are too small to absorb the scope of the privatization plans of countries like France or Italy. Thus, deregulating domestic financial markets and allowing greater foreign participation is a necessary step in the privatization process.

Product Innovation and Volatility

The massive increase in the levels of volatility experienced in stock, bond, and foreign exchange markets since the early 1970s is one of

Table 18.1   Imports as a percentage of GNP: A comparison across countries, 1965–1985

	USA	Japan	Canada	Germany	UK	Italy	France
1965	4.7	7.5	12.5	12.8	15.0	9.8	8.8
1966	5.1	7.5	13.0	12.4	14.7	10.6	9.3
1967	5.2	7.9	13.1	11.9	15.0	11.0	9.0
1968	5.5	7.4	13.7	12.7	17.1	10.6	9.3
1969	5.7	7.3	14.2	13.7	17.1	11.6	10.5
1970	6.0	7.7	13.1	13.5	17.0	12.4	10.6
1971	6.0	7.1	13.4	13.3	16.1	12.0	10.5
1972	6.4	6.5	14.3	13.0	16.3	12.5	10.8
1973	7.2	7.7	15.3	13.2	19.7	15.1	11.6
1974	9.2	11.2	17.4	15.2	25.0	20.1	15.6
1975	8.2	9.7	16.9	14.9	20.8	16.7	12.7
1976	8.9	9.6	15.8	16.4	22.5	19.5	14.6
1977	9.5	8.6	16.2	16.3	23.4	18.6	14.6
1978	9.9	6.8	17.3	15.7	22.0	17.9	13.8
1979	10.9	9.1	19.0	17.4	22.7	19.9	14.9
1980	11.7	11.1	18.6	19.2	20.8	21.0	16.6
1981	11.4	10.2	18.6	19.9	19.5	21.5	16.8
1982	10.6	10.1	15.1	19.6	20.1	20.6	17.0
1983	10.5	8.9	15.5	19.4	21.1	18.8	16.4
1984	11.7	9.0	17.9	20.6	23.5	20.1	17.0
1985	11.2	8.2	18.4	21.0	23.3	21.0	16.9

the major forces driving product innovation in financial markets. Investors and corporations have learned to cope with the higher risks implied by these volatile times with an array of risk management products, including financial futures, options, warrants, floating rate bonds, bonds with rate caps, equity convertibles, and a myriad of other financial instruments.

The financial volatility that spurred much of this new product development, however, could well be on the decrease. Markets without volatility do not need options and risk management products because of the lack of risk.

The most important development suggesting that financial volatility could drop sharply in the years ahead has to do with the war against inflation. A good case can be made that this war has been won. In figure 18.2 the rate of wholesale price inflation in the United States, Germany, and Japan in 1980 is contrasted with that in 1986. If anything, deflation has replaced inflation. Wholesale prices, however, have always been more volatile than consumer

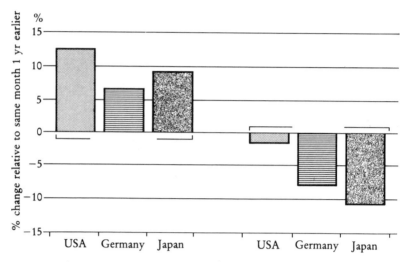

Figure 18.2   Wholesale price inflation, 1980 vs. 1986

prices. What the deflation in wholesale prices means is that an important milestone in establishing stable consumer prices has been achieved. Table 18.2 shows the rates of consumer price inflation for the four years 1983–6, and illustrates the impressive progress that has been made toward price stability.

Table 18.2   Average annual CPI inflation, 1971–1986

	1971–82	1983	1984	1985	1986
United States	7.9	3.2	4.3	3.5	1.9
Japan	8.1	1.9	2.2	2.1	0.0
Germany	5.2	3.3	2.4	2.2	−0.5
France	10.1	9.6	7.4	5.8	2.0
United Kingdom	13.1	4.6	5.0	6.1	3.0
Italy	14.4	14.6	10.8	9.2	6.0

Because inflation distorts the price signals upon which free-market economies depend to efficiently allocate goods, services, and capital, inflation is a critical factor in the volatility question. When prices are rising rapidly, it is very difficult to tell whether a good is becoming relatively expensive or whether the prices of all goods are rising. In making business plans, investment decisions, and the like, being able to distinguish between a change in relative prices and general inflation makes all the difference in the world. Inflation, by distorting that information, creates volatility; people make more mistakes, then they have to correct the errors – and mistakes slow economic growth. Table 18.3 compares economic growth rates in the stable 1960s versus the more volatile 1970s and 1980s, and the shift to slower world growth is quite apparent.

Table 18.3   Annual average real GNP growth rates, 1961–1985

	1961–70	1971–80	1981–85
France	5.6	3.6	1.1
Germany	4.5	2.7	1.2
Italy	5.7	3.2	0.9
Japan	11.7	4.7	3.9
United Kingdom	3.0	1.8	1.9
United States	3.9	3.1	2.3

The case that the back of inflation has been broken does not rest on the collapse of oil prices in 1986, but is more properly viewed as a permanent shift in economic policy-making. Starting in the early 1980s, a much more restrictive, non-inflationary policy stance was adopted in many industrialized nations. Germany and Japan moved to conservative fiscal policies, as shown in table 18.4. The United States ran expansionary fiscal programs, but offset them with restrictive monetary policies, as is evidenced by relatively high real interest rates. In short, five years of conservative policy management around the world has laid a firm base for a new non-inflationary environment.

Table 18.4   Federal plus state and local government budget balances as a percentage of nominal GNP, 1980–1985

	1980	1981	1982	1983	1984	1985
Germany	−2.9	−3.7	−3.3	−2.5	−1.9	−1.1
Japan	−4.4	−3.9	−3.6	−3.7	−2.2	−1.3
United States	−1.3	−1.0	−3.5	−3.8	−2.9	−3.5

Source: Organization for Economic Cooperation and Development, *Economic Outlook*, May 1986.

Of course, there are still some backsliding countries, which are threatening to give away the gains. And world markets in stocks, bonds, and foreign exchange are still trying to assess the probabilities that the world is, indeed, entering a new phase. So the era of volatility is not over yet, but the signs of substantial, fundamental change are present.

If the next ten years exhibit greater price stability, the implications will be almost as revolutionary as the shift to inflation and volatility that occurred in the 1980s. Product innovation may well continue, but the products will be very different. No longer will financial risk management be the key to success. Instead, financial products will be tailored to the specific income-generating capabilities of the underlying investment project. This means that the days when corporations could make money on creative financing strategies without having a strong business plan are over. Investors will have to worry more about corporate business plans and less about inflation-induced volatility. And an entire industry of financial engineers with specialities in volatility management will need to learn new trades.

Securitization and Re-regulation

As we have seen, the process of packaging financial instruments in standard forms and then buying and selling these instruments is known as securitization. The process is perhaps best seen in the mortgage industry (covered in chapter 14), with the development of mortgage pass-through securities and collateralized mortgage obligations (CMOs). Securitization, however, has affected many other financial markets, from car loans to the bank debt of developing countries, as the financial firms making the original loans have sought to package them and sell them to someone else.

Securitization is a part of the product innovation revolution discussed in the previous section and some of the impetus for securitization has come from market volatility. But there have been other causes for this trend that are equally important. As noted in the introduction to this volume, the institutionalization trend – the growth of investable money under institutional management by pension funds, insurance companies, and the like – has created a dominant and extremely sophisticated investor base. These institutions have been willing to take the time and spend the required effort to understand the new products, assessing their risk (and risk-reducing) characteristics. There are no signs that the trend of institutionalization is waning, and the appetite and willingness of institutional fund managers for securitized products should remain very strong.

An attack on securitization, however, may emerge from another source: from central banks and financial regulators. Always known to be 'party-poopers,' this group of regulators is increasingly concerned that the proliferation of securitized products carries with it an increased risk to the world's financial system.

The potential system-wide risks from securitization bear in no small part on the structural changes that this trend has wrought on the banking system and the resulting shifts of power in regulatory circles. The securitization process weakens the role of commercial banks in the monetary system. And a reduced role for commercial banks weakens the power of bank regulators. Let us explain.

Commercial banks were once the main purveyors of credit risk assessment. Banks evaluated potential creditors and made loans. The loans were funded by deposits gathered from consumers and corporations. Banks functioned as both financial and credit intermediaries; that is, they were the middlemen in the economy-wide process of borrowing and lending money and in assessing credit risk. By regulating banks, central bank and monetary authorities could influence, in a broad sense, financial developments in an economy.

Securitization is a symptom, however, of the reduced role of commercial banks in the functioning of the world's economies. The large money management institutions are fully capable of assessing credit risk. Large corporations may have credit ratings that equal banks and can now raise funds directly from institutional investors. The role of the middleman in financial intermediation and in credit risk assessment has thus, been reduced dramatically. Securitization is the messenger of that process.

A major implication is that the ability of the monetary authorities to regulate banks no longer implies as much control over the economy as it once did. Furthermore, monetary authorities, *de facto*, are having to share economic influence and power with the national bodies that regulate stock markets, pension funds, futures markets, and so on.

In short, what we have here is the making of a classic power struggle. Regulators from different government agencies are going to be reassessing their influence, reassessing more generally the proper methods of influencing financial markets, and, no doubt, fighting among themselves for turf and the right to regulate this new financial environment. Part of this fight for regulatory authority is very likely to lead to a slow process of re-regulation.

A developing trend toward re-regulation will almost certainly slow the securitization process. This does not mean that the market for securitized products will decline, because the institutionalization trend is too entrenched for that to happen. Rather, securitized products will simply face increased regulation and scrutiny from the monetary authorities, with the likely imposition of various capital ratios, exposure limitations, and so on being applied to certain products and their use.

Evolution or a New Revolution?

The discussion so far has sought to challenge the fashionable idea that the themes of the mid-1970s to mid-1980s – globalization, product innovation, and securitization – will simply shift from revolutionary change to a pattern of relatively smooth evolution. Most likely, however, developments will not work that way. A number of critical factors are emerging that have the potential to shift dramatically the direction from which the winds of change are blowing. These factors – trade protectionism, reduced financial market volatility with more stable price levels, and re-regulation – well may be as important to the next decade as the forces of technology, institutionalization, and market volatility were to the last decade, as was emphasized in this volume's introduction.

Moreover, these new trends suggest that life on Wall Street in the next decade may not be a bed of evolutionary roses. Changing environments require changing strategies. And as the forces that have brought explosive growth to Wall Street subside and new forces point in different directions, the adaptation process will begin again. Some firms will emerge stronger and more profitable. Others will be bought and merged; and, yes, some may fail. For Wall Street, this is no time to let one's guard down and assume smooth, evolutionary growth. The winds of change are blowing again – from new directions.

Glossary of Terms

Asymmetrical risk
Applies to an asset that has uneven potential for gains and losses; that is, the probability distribution of returns is skewed in either a positive or a negative direction. A call option is one example of an asset with an asymmetrical risk distribution, since it has virtually unlimited up-side potential but the down-side risk is limited to the premium paid for the option.

Basis risk
With respect to futures contracts, the 'basis' represents the difference between the price of the cash commodity and a related futures contract, a difference that widens or narrows as the cash and futures prices fluctuate. Basis risk refers to the possibility that this difference will change during the life of the contract, resulting in an unexpected loss or gain. The basis is the determinant of profit or loss in hedging; if it remains constant over the life of a position, a perfect hedge (losses exactly equal to gains) results. Basis risk also results when a particular futures contract is used to hedge a portfolio that differs from the underlying futures instrument.

Beta
The regression coefficient for the rate of return on the market in the following market model equation:

$$Security\ return = a + beta \times (market\ return) + e$$

where a is a constant and e is an error term with an expected value of zero. Beta measures the sensitivity of the return of a particular security (or portfolio) to the return of the market as a whole. A beta of 1.0 indicates that, if the market experiences a 1 percent increase in return, the security (or portfolio) in question will also experience a 1 percent increase in return. Similarly, a security with a beta of, say, 0.8 will increase/decrease by only 0.8 percent for every 1 percent increase/decrease in the market and is therefore considered to be less risky than the market. An estimate of the beta coefficient for a portfolio is the weighted average of the betas of the components of the portfolio.

Bid–ask spread

The difference between the prices quoted by a dealer or specialist for buying (bid) and selling (ask) a security.

Callable bond

A bond with a call provision, which gives the issuer the right to redeem the bonds under specified terms prior to the normal maturity date. The call price is equal to the par value plus a call premium.

Collateralized mortgage obligations (CMOs)

When a financial institution puts together a group of mortgages into one security, one form that this security can take is that of a collateralized mortgage obligation (CMO). The CMO structure is a classic example of securitization, (q.v.). In essence, there has been created a family of mutual funds that invest only in mortgages. Hence, the funds hold the mortgages as collateral. Furthermore, the way that the interest and principal is distributed to investors is segregated among the funds into different tranches (members of the family) of the CMO, with different expected maturities. Pieces of CMOs are actively traded on Wall Street and have brought a great deal of liquidity and flexibility to the mortgage market.

Company-specific risk

See 'Unsystematic risk.'

Cost of capital

The discount rate that should be used in the process of evaluating capital projects or acquisitions.

Credit risk

The risk that an individual, firm, or nation will not meet its financial obligations in full and on time. The concept is broader than bankruptcy risk, which is the ultimate in credit failure, and embodies a judgement concerning the potential for late payments as well as default.

Credit spread
The interest rate differential between two securities of identical terms and maturity, whose only difference lies in the markets' perception of the relative credit risk of the borrowers. For example, on a ten-year, non-callable bond, the US Treasury would pay a lower interest rate than an automobile company or a steel company, based on the market's judgement that the US Treasury is a better credit risk than the other borrowers.

Discount issue yield
The yield received on a note at the date of issue as represented by the discount between the purchase price and the face value of the note.

Discount rate
In corporate finance, the interest rate used in the discounting process; in analyzing economic trends, the interest rate charged by the central bank (Federal Reserve) to commercial banks.

Diversification
The spreading of investments over more than one company, industry, currency, etc., to reduce the uncertainty of future returns caused by unsystematic risk. In a large, diverse portfolio, therefore, certain risks can be expected to offset each other.

Duration
A measure used to describe the price sensitivity of a coupon bond to a given interest rate change which takes into account both the maturity and the coupon rate of the bond. The duration calculation converts a coupon bond to its zero-coupon bond equivalent by finding the amount of time (in months or years) that must pass before the coupon reinvestment effects of a change in interest rates offset the price (principal) risk of selling the remaining life of a bond. The duration of a coupon bond is less than its maturity; the duration of a zero coupon bond is equal to its maturity.

Earnings per share (EPS)
A financial measure computed by dividing the income available to common shares by the number of outstanding common shares. Income must be adjusted for preferred dividends, and the potential dilutive effects of outstanding convertible preferred stocks must also be considered.

Eurobond
A bond sold in a country other than the one in whose currency the bond is denominated.

Eurodollar
A time deposit in a foreign bank (or foreign branch of a US bank) which is denominated in US dollars.

Euromarket
In financial jargon, the prefix 'Euro' has come to mean any market or product that is developed and trades outside traditional national boundaries and domestic regulations, regardless of whether the activity is in Europe, Singapore, or the Cayman Islands. For instance, the Eurodollar market is the generic name for the trading of dollar bank deposits outside the United States, mostly by large international banks. The most active Eurobanking center is London, but Caribbean centers such as the Bahamas or the Cayman Islands exist as well. Another example would be the issuance of bonds – 'Eurobonds' – in London by US multinational companies without the filing of the traditional set of documents required by the US Securities and Exchange Commission.

Euronote
A fully negotiable bearer promissory note which is sold in a country other than the one in whose currency the note is denominated. Euronotes are usually issued at a discount to face value and are typically short-term of one, three, or six months' maturity.

Expected return
The return that is expected to be realized from an asset or portfolio. It is the weighted arithmetic average of all possible outcomes, where the weights represent the probability that each outcome will occur.

Federal funds
Assets of depository institutions that represent a designated fraction of their demand and time deposit liabilities that are required to be held on reserve with a district Federal Reserve Bank in the form of interest-free deposits. Excess reserves can be lent, usually on a very short-term basis, to other commercial banks desiring to borrow them.

Federal funds rate
The interest rate charged on federal funds borrowings.

Federal Reserve discount rate
The rate charged by the Federal Reserve for loans made to depository institutions.

FIFO (first-in, first-out)
An inventory costing method where unit costs enter the cost of goods sold in the same order in which they enter the cost of goods available. In periods of rising prices, FIFO produces a larger gross margin and a greater net income by reporting a lower cost of goods sold compared with other methods.

Forward contract
An agreement privately negotiated between a buyer and a seller to deliver a specified amount of a cash commodity at an agreed-upon time and delivery point. The price may be agreed upon when the transaction is entered into or determined at the time of delivery.

Futures contract
A commitment to buy or sell a fixed amount of a specific product for delivery at a predetermined future date at a price that is determined on the date the contract is made. Unlike forward contracts, futures contracts are traded on designated futures contract markets and are uniform with respect to the quantity, quality, and delivery of a specified underlying product. The buyer or seller of a futures contract is required to make only a small initial margin deposit, and each position is 'marked to market' on a daily basis and the investors' account debited or credited to reflect changes in value. Additional margin is required if the investor's account falls below a specified level.

Goodwill
The intangible assets of a firm represented by the excess of the price paid for a going concern over the value of its assets.

Hurdle rate
In capital budgeting, the minimum acceptable rate of return on a project. If the expected rate of return is below this rate, the project is not acceptable. The hurdle rate should be the risk-adjusted marginal cost of capital.

Immunization
A technique that attempts to eliminate the sensitivity of a portfolio of bonds to reinvestment risk over a specific period of time.

Indexation
An investment process which creates a portfolio designed to match the returns of a chosen market index such as the Standard & Poors' 500. Index funds can be created in a number of ways. In a census approach, all members are held in proportions roughly identical to the target index. In a stratified sample approach, the target index is divided by industry or market capitalization, and a sample of stocks within each strata is owned. A third strategy, called 'portfolio optimization,' uses econometric techniques to find an appropriate subset of securities to track the index.

Institutionalization
As workers have been granted increasingly better pensions, large amounts of money have accumulated in pension funds. The size of the funds under professional management now allows institutions to dominate individual investors in the stock and bond markets. This process is known as institutionalization.

Law of diminishing returns
A law stating that, as one continues a particular activity, the returns from that activity for a given unit of effort eventually begin to decline. For example, a firm in the computer industry may face an array of very profitable projects in which to invest, but as projects are completed, the new projects offer less and less potential. Diminishing returns have set in.

LIFO (last-in, first-out)
An inventory costing method where unit costs enter the cost of goods sold in the reverse of the order in which they enter the cost of goods available.

Liquidity premium
Normally, the degree by which prices are reduced and interest rates raised because a fixed-income security is not easily traded. That is, the market for the security may not be deep, and may involve only a few investors and traders, such that the sale of the security can take time. To accelerate the process, a liquidity premium is offered in terms of a lower price and a higher interest rate. Secondarily, the term sometimes refers to the increased riskiness of long-term fixed-income securities. The argument is made that investors are willing to pay a premium (lower interest rates) for shorter-term investments. Hence, the normal shape of the yield curve is positively sloped, with lower short-term interest rates than long-term rates.

Market efficiency
A hypothesis that security prices fully reflect all available information and that adjustments to new information are virtually instantaneous.

Market risk
See 'Systematic risk.'

Monetarist
Strictly speaking, a person who believes that the primary determinant of inflation in the future is the growth rate of a nation's money stock. More broadly, the term encompasses a wide variety of economic thought which views monetary policy as the critical force in influencing inflation and related financial variables, such as interest rates and exchange rates.

Mortgage-backed securities
When a US savings and loan institution or a commercial bank originates a mortgage to a homeowner, these institutions often group or pool the mortgages and form a mortgage-backed security. The individual mortgages, collateralized by housing stock, represent the assets of this new mortgage-backed security, which is then sold whole or in pieces on Wall Street. Such a

security allows many types of investors to participate in the home mortgage market without being involved in the mechanics of making the loans, and with the added benefit of risk diversification, by having a small share in many mortgages rather than being locked into one mortgage.

Nominal return

The rate of return on an asset in monetary terms, or unadjusted for inflation. This is contrasted with the real return (q.v.), which is adjusted for changes in the price level.

Open-market operations

The purchase or sale of US securities by the Federal Reserve system for the purpose of altering the amount of member bank reserves. The Open Market Committee has the responsibility for determining the direction and extent of open-market operations which are binding on all Federal Reserve banks.

Opportunity cost

The rate of return on the best *alternative* investment available, or the highest return that will *not* be earned if funds are invested in a particular project or security.

Option

An 'option contract' is the right to buy or sell securities or commodities as a specified price (the exercise price) on or before a given date (the expiration date or maturity date). Options to purchase securities are termed 'calls'; options to sell are known as 'puts.' The individual issuing an option is called the 'seller' or 'writer' and the individual purchasing the option is called the 'buyer.' An American option may be exercised on or before the expiration date; a European option can be exercised only at expiration. Options granted by corporations are known as 'warrants' or 'rights.'

Present value

The actual value of a payment or stream of payments discounted at an appropriate rate of interest. The present value of an asset depends on the amounts of future cash flows, their timing, the interest rate used to discount them, and the length of the compounding interval.

Price–earnings (PE) ratio
A financial measure computed by dividing the market price per share of common stock at a specific date by the annual earnings per share. Comparisons of PE ratios between companies in the same industry, and with industry averages, are often used as a tool by investors in evaluating investment opportunities.

Price risk
The potential for capital gains or losses from selling the remaining life of a bond after a change in interest rates.

Principal risk
A risk that a bond's price will rise or fall in value if interest rates change.

Random walk
A term implying that there is no discernible pattern of travel. The last step, or even all the previous steps, cannot be used to predict either the size or the direction of the next step.

Rational expectations
A concept implying that the market forms expectations in a way that is consistent with the actual economic structure of the market. The prices that result in the marketplace represent an average of all investors' expectations.

Real interest rate
The difference between the interest rate on a relatively credit-risk-free security, such as US Treasury bonds, and the expected inflation rate over the maturity period of the bond in question. The term 'real' in economic jargon means inflation-adjusted. In this case, interest rates are being reduced by the loss of purchasing power resulting from inflation.

Real return
The rate of return as an asset after adjusting for inflation.

Refinance option
When a loan is made at a fixed interest rate for a fixed maturity, the lender may negotiate a refinance option with the borrower. This allows the borrower to refinance the loan at a lower interest rate if, at some future date, interest rates have moved to lower

levels. For example, most home mortgages in the United States allow the borrower to prepay his fixed-rate loan with no penalty. Thus, when interest rates fell in 1985 and 1986, many home-owners exercised their options and refinanced their mortgages at lower interest rates.

Reinvestment risk
The risk that cash flows (coupon payments) received from a coupon bond will be reinvested at uncertain future interest rates.

Required return
The rate of return that stockholders expect to receive on common stock investments. This is determined by making comparisons with alternative investments (such as bonds) after adjusting for differences in risk.

Risk
The probability that actual realized returns will not equal expected returns. This is often measured by the standard deviation of expected returns, or by the beta coefficient.

Risk structure
Portfolios contain different levels and types of risks. Risk structure is a broad concept which embodies the risks in a given portfolio and how the individual risks in the portfolio may be offset or be associated with each other.

Securitization
The process of packaging assets and liabilities such that they can be sold and resold (traded) in active markets. This allows the financial institution that originates the deal – a mortgage, a car loan, etc. – to sell the asset to other investors, thus freeing the capital of the originator for alternative uses. Excellent examples of securitization are in the mortgage-backed securities (q.v.) family, where individual homeowner mortgages are made by savings and loan institutions, pooled into large groups, and sold to Wall Street institutions, who then sell pieces of the whole package to pension funds and other large investors, who in turn actively trade these securitized products – in this case, pieces of mortgages.

Standard deviation
A statistical measurement of the variability of a set of observa-

tions. This is a commonly used measure of dispersion based on the deviations of observations from the mean.

Symmetrical risk
An asset that has a normal, or symmetrical, distribution of possible returns.

Systematic risk
The volatility of rates of return on stocks or portfolios in relation to changes in rates of return on the whole market. Also known as 'market risk,' it stems from such things as war, inflation, recessions, and high interest rates. Since these are factors that affect all firms simultaneously, this type of risk cannot be eliminated by diversification. Systematic or market risk is measured by the beta coefficient (see *Beta*).

Takeover
The acquisition of one firm by another over the opposition of the acquired firm's management.

Technical analysis
An approach to forecasting prices based on past and present market activity and not on fundamental economic judgements.

Tender offer
A situation where one company offers to purchase the stock of another by going directly to the stockholders, frequently over the opposition of the management of the target company.

Unsystematic risk
That part of a security's risk associated with random events. Also known as 'company-specific risk,' it refers to such things as lawsuits, strikes, successful and unsuccessful marketing programs, fire, and other events that are unique to a particular firm. Since these events are essentially random, their effects on a portfolio can be eliminated by diversification. (q.v.)

Warrant
A long-term option to buy a stated number of shares of common stock at a specified price (known as the 'exercise price').

Yield curve

A graph of the relationship between the yields and the maturities of a security. The yield curve can be positive, negative, or flat, reflecting higher, lower, or equal yields (respectively) as the maturity lengthens.

Zero-coupon bond

A bond that pays no periodic interest, but sells at a discount below par and therefore provides compensation to investors in the form of capital appreciation.

List of Figures

List of Tables

Index

Note: References are to United States, unless otherwise indicated.

repackaging, 4
required returns, 204
re-regulation, 192–4
restructuring, corporate, 6
  see also acquisitions
returns
  after-tax rate of, 65, 92
  anticipated, 84
  expected, 113, 198
  law of diminishing, 47–8, 57, 200
  nominal, 202
  real, 113, 203
  required, 204
  see also dividends; economic
    returns; yield and under risk
risk, 2–6, 204
  assessment, 178, 182
  basis 153–6, 195
  corporations and, 15–18, 58–9
  credit, 117, 131, 137, 196–7
  currencies, 176–83
    fiscal policy, 181–3
    inflation, and 178–9
    trade and external balance,
      179–81
  defined, 13
  dividends and, 89–90
  hedges and, 153–7
    basic, 153–6
  inflation, and currencies, 3, 178–9
  management, 142
    see also interest rate risk
  market, 58, 201
  -neutral, 167
  principal versus reinvestment,
    121–2
  real interest rates and, 117
  reinvestment, 107, 204
    versus principal risk, 121–2
  and return, 8, 13–24
    asymmetry, 13, 20–3, 158, 195
    avoidable, 13, 16–24
    see also beta and currencies
      above
  shifting see securitization
  stock prices and, 85

structure, 204
symmetrical, 20, 205
systematic, 205
unsystematic 208
  see also under interest rates
rollover strategy, 107, 150
Rosenberg, B., 19
Rudd, A., 19

S & P see Standard and Poors
St Joe, 69
Sears, 69
Securities Exchange Commission
  (SEC), 28, 61
securitization, 3–4, 204
  and re-regulation, 192–4
  see also under mortgage
Shearson Lehmann, 1
short-run theories of real interest
  rates, 116
Singapore, 166
Sinquefield, R.A., 54
size of corporations see large
Sohio, 69
Southern Pacific, 76
spot markets, 167, 169
Sprint, 69, 76
stand-alone value of target
  companies, 70–1, 73, 74, 76
standard deviation, 204–5
Standard and Poors, 133
  500 Index, 7, 21
star, fallen, 133
statistics see communications;
  information
Stern, J., 27, 61n, 78n, 95n
Stewart, B., 61n, 68n, 78n
stock/stock market, 9
  driven by bond market, 95–101
  and acquisitions, 69–70
  case studies (1982–3 &
    1985–6), 97–101
  opportunity cost of
    investment, 95–6
  stocks versus bonds, 55, 56,
    96–7

*Index compiled by
Ann Hall*

About the Authors

Bluford H. Putnam

Bluford H. Putnam is a Principal with Morgan Stanley & Company. He formed and heads the firm's international fixed income strategy team, with responsibilities for analysis and portfolio recommendations involving global bond and currency markets. He joined Morgan Stanley in 1984 as the firm's senior international economist. Previously, he was Chief Economist and partner with Stern Stewart & Company (1982–84), a vice president with the Chase Manhattan Bank (1978–82), and an economist with the Federal Reserve Bank of New York (1976–77).

He holds a Ph.D. in Economics from Tulane University (New Orleans LA.) and a B.A. from Eckerd College (St. Petersburg, FL.). He has published extensively in academic research journals and in the business press, as well as edited two books on international financial markets. He currently serves on the adjunct faculty of Columbia University.

Sandra C. Zimmer

Sandra C. Zimmer is a second vice president with the Treasury Department of the Chase Manhattan Bank. She serves in the special projects division, which develops new financial products. Prior to this assignment, she held portfolio and marketing responsibilities in the Indexing and Hedging Group of the Chase Investors Management Corporation (a wholly owned subsidiary of the Chase Manhattan Bank). She joined the Chase Manhattan Bank in 1980 in the Economics Department and was a member of the team that designed, developed, and implemented the financial risk management training and marketing programs of the Chase Development Institute.

She holds a B.A. in Economics from Eckerd College (St. Petersburg, FL.) and has done graduate work in finance at New York University.